THOMAS
HARDY

COMPREHENSIVE RESEARCH
AND STUDY GUIDE

BLOOM'S
MAJOR
NOVELISTS

EDITED AND WITH AN
INTRODUCTION BY HAROLD BLOOM

THOMAS
HARDY

COMPREHENSIVE RESEARCH
AND STUDY GUIDE

BLOOM'S

MAJOR
NOVELISTS

EDITED AND WITH AN INTRODUCTION
BY HAROLD BLOOM

CHELSEA HOUSE
PUBLISHERS
A Haights Cross Communications Company
Philadelphia

First Printing
1 3 5 7 9 8 6 4 2

Library of Congress Cataloging-in-Publication Data

Thomas Hardy / edited and with an introduction by Harold Bloom.
    p. cm. — (Bloom's major novelists)
  Includes bibliographical references and index.
  ISBN 0-7910-6348-8
  1. Hardy, Thomas, 1840–1928—Fictional works. 2. Wessex
(England)—In literature. I. Bloom, Harold. II. Series.
PR4754 .T46 2002
823'.8—dc21
                        2002151007

Chelsea House Publishers
1974 Sproul Road, Suite 400
Broomall, PA 19008-0914

www.chelseahouse.com

Contributing Editor: Janyce Marson

Produced by: www.bookdesigning.com

Cover design by Robert Gerson

Contents

User's Guide

This volume is designed to present biographical, critical, and bibliographical information on the author's best-known or most important works. Following Harold Bloom's editor's note and introduction is a detailed biography of the author, discussing major life events and important literary accomplishments. A plot summary of each novel follows, tracing significant themes, patterns, and motifs in the work.

A selection of critical extracts, derived from previously published material from leading critics, analyzes aspects of each work. The extracts consist of statements from the author, if available, early reviews of the work, and later evaluations up to the present. A bibliography of the author's writings (including a complete list of all works written, cowritten, edited, and translated), a list of additional books and articles on the author and his or her work, and an index of themes and ideas in the author's writings conclude the volume.

~

Harold Bloom is Sterling Professor of the Humanities at Yale University and Henry W. and Albert A. Berg Professor of English at the New York University Graduate School. He is the author of over 20 books, including *Shelley's Mythmaking* (1959), *The Visionary Company* (1961), *Blake's Apocalypse* (1963), *Yeats* (1970), *A Map of Misreading* (1975), *Kabbalah and Criticism* (1975), *Agon: Toward a Theory of Revisionism* (1982), *The American Religion* (1992), *The Western Canon* (1994), and *Omens of Millennium: The Gnosis of Angels, Dreams, and Resurrection* (1996). *The Anxiety of Influence* (1973) sets forth Professor Bloom's provocative theory of the literary relationships between the great writers and their predecessors. His most recent books include *Shakespeare: The Invention of the Human*, a 1998 National Book Award finalist, and *How to Read and Why*, which was published in 2000.

Professor Bloom earned his Ph.D. from Yale University in 1955 and has served on the Yale faculty since then. He is a 1985 MacArthur Foundation Award recipient, served as the Charles Eliot Norton Professor of Poetry at Harvard University in 1987–88, and has received honorary degrees from the universities of Rome and Bologna. In 1999, Professor Bloom received the prestigious American Academy of Arts and Letters Gold Medal for Criticism.

Currently, Harold Bloom is the editor of numerous Chelsea House volumes of literary criticism, including the series BLOOM'S NOTES, BLOOM'S MAJOR DRAMATISTS, BLOOM'S MAJOR NOVELISTS, MAJOR LITERARY CHARACTERS, BLOOM'S MODERN CRITICAL VIEWS, BLOOM'S MODERN CRITICAL INTERPRETATIONS, and WOMEN WRITERS OF ENGLISH AND THEIR WORKS.

Editor's Note

My Introduction remarks upon Hardy's affinity with Walter Pater, and meditates briefly on the enchanting Eustacia Vye, Queen of Night in *The Return of the Native*.

As this volume excerpts over twenty-five Critical Views in relation to five novels, I am obliged to be highly selective in calling attention to a small selection among them.

On *Far from the Madding Crowd*, Howard Babb sets the context, and Judith Bryant Wittenberg analyzes multiple perspectives.

My personal favorites among Hardy's novels are *The Woodlanders* and *The Return of the Native*, the latter of which is illuminated in regard to plot by Gillian Beer, after which Robert Langbaum considers Hardy's vision of pastoral, and Perry Meisel brilliantly uncovers the novel's Freudian dynamic.

The Mayor of Casterbridge, a tragic triumph, is compared by R. P. Draper to the story of Oedipus, while Michael Taft invokes folklore.

Another powerful tragedy, *Tess of the d'Urbervilles*, is investigated by Mary Jacobus and by Lisa Sternlieb in regard to Biblical analogues.

Jude the Obscure, Hardy's most controversial novel, has Sue Bridehead as its equivocal glory. She is interpreted here by Elizabeth Langland, while Paul Pickrel helpfully invokes the Fall of Phaethon as a guide to Jude's ruin.

Introduction

HAROLD BLOOM

Thomas Hardy lived to be eighty-seven and a half years old, and his long life (1840–1928) comprised two separate literary careers, as a late Victorian novelist (1871–1897), and as a poet who defies temporal placement (1898–1928). The critical reaction to his final novels, *The Well-Beloved* and *Jude the Obscure,* ostensibly motivated Hardy's abandonment of prose fiction, but he always had thought of himself as a poet, and by 1897 was financially secure enough to center himself upon his poetry. He is—with Housman, Yeats, D. H. Lawrence, Wilfred Owen, and Geoffrey Hill—one of the half-dozen or so major poets of the British Isles in the century just past. But this little volume concerns itself with several of his best novels, where again he can be judged to be one of the crucial novelists of the final three decades of the nineteenth century, the bridge connecting George Eliot and the Brontës to Lawrence's novels in the earlier twentieth-century.

   T. S. Eliot, who continues to enjoy a high critical reputation despite being almost always wrong, attacked Hardy in a dreadful polemic, *After Strange Gods,* where the novelist-poet is stigmatized as not believing in Original Sin, which turns out to be an aesthetic criterion, since Hardy's style "touches sublimity without ever having passed through the stage of being good." This inaccurate wisecrack is prompted by Eliot's severe summary of the post-Protestant Hardy: "A powerful personality uncurbed by any institutional attachment or by submission to any objective beliefs; unhampered by any ideas." Eliot's institutional attachment was to the Anglo-Catholic Church: his "objective beliefs" were Christianity, royalism, and what he called "classicism" and his "ideas" excluded Freud and Marx.

   Hardy, as High Romantic as Shelley and the Brontës, or as Lawrence and Yeats, cannot be judged by Neo-Christian ideology. The best books upon him remain, in my judgment, Lionel Johnson's early *The Art of Thomas Hardy,* and D. H. Lawrence's outrageous *A Study of Thomas Hardy*—which is mostly about Hardy's impact on Lawrence. Michael Millgate's remains the best biography, but since Hardy burned letters and concealed relationships, we still do not know enough to fully integrate the work and the life. Both of

Hardy's marriages evidently did not fulfill him, and his lifelong attraction to women much younger than himself has an Ibsenite and Yeatsian aura to it. There is a dark intensity, in the novels and poems alike, that has marked sado-masochistic overtones.

Hardy's personal greatness as a novelist is enhanced (and enabled) by his freedom from T. S. Eliot's attachments and submissions. The agnostic Hardy was Schopenhauerian before he read Schopenhauer, and found a name for the Will to Live that destroys the protagonists of his novels. Hardy's women and men are driven by the tragic forces that are incarnated in Sophocles's Electra, Shakespeare's Lear and Macbeth, and Tolstoy's Anna Karenina. Henry James, who regarded Hardy as a poor imitator of George Eliot, was as mistaken as T. S. Eliot was after him. D. H. Lawrence, in his *Study of Thomas Hardy,* was much more accurate:

> And this is the quality Hardy shares with the great writers, Shakespeare or Sophocles or Tolstoi, this setting behind the small action of his protagonists the terrific action of unfathomed nature; setting a smaller system of morality, the one grasped and formulated by the human consciousness. The difference is, that whereas in Shakespeare or Sophocles the greater, uncomprehended morality, or fate, is actively transgressed, and holds, and punishes the protagonist, whilst the greater morality is only passively, negatively transgressed, it is represented merely as being present in background, in scenery, not taking any active part, having no direct connexion with the protagonist. Oedipus, Hamlet, Macbeth set themselves up against, or find themselves set up against, the unfathomed moral forces of nature, and out of this unfathomed force comes their death. Whereas Anna Karenina, Eustacia, Tess, Sue, and Jude find themselves up against the established system of human government and morality, they cannot detach themselves, and are brought down. Their real tragedy is that they are unfaithful to the greater unwritten morality, which would have bidden Anna Karenina be patient and wait until she, by virtue of greater right, could take what she needed from society; would have bidden Vronsky detach himself from the system, become an individual, creating a new colony of morality with Anna; would have bidden Eustacia fight Clym for his own soul, and Tess take and claim her Angel, since she had the greater light; would

have bidden Jude and Sue endure for very honour's sake, since one must bide by the best that one has known, and not succumb to the lesser good.

What matters most, in Hardy's women and men, is their tragic dignity, though their author denies them the ultimate freedom of choice. Hardy's chief limitation, as a novelist, is his sense that the will is over-determined, as it is in Schopenhauer. What saves Hardy's novels is that pragmatically he cannot maintain the detachment he seeks in regard to his central personages. I recall, at fifteen, first reading *The Return of the Native*, and falling-in-love with a second Hardy heroine, thus becoming unfaithful to my love, Marty South in *The Woodlanders*. Hardy himself was ambivalent towards Eustacia Vye, and yet he invokes her as a goddess, Queen of Night, in a rhapsody not less than astonishing:

Eustacia Vye was the raw material of a divinity. On Olympus she would have done well with a little preparation. She had the passions and instincts which make a model goddess, that is, those which make not quite a model woman. Had it been possible for the earth and mankind to be entirely in her grasp for a while, had she handled the distaff, the spindle, and the shears at her own free will, few in the world would have noticed the change of government. There would have been the same inequality of lot, the same heaping up of favours here, of contumely there, the same generosity before justice, the same perpetual dilemmas, the same captious alternation of caresses and blows that we endure now.

She was in person full-limbed and somewhat heavy; without ruddiness, as without pallor; and soft to the touch as a cloud. To see her hair was to fancy that a whole winter did not contain darkness enough to form its shadow: it closed over her forehead like nightfall extinguishing the western glow.

Her nerves extended into those tresses, and her temper could always be softened by stroking them down. When her hair was brushed she would instantly sink into stillness and look like the Sphinx. If, in passing under one of the Egdon banks, any of its thick skeins were caught, as they sometimes were, by a prickly tuft of the large *Ulex Europoeus*—which will act as a sort of hairbrush—she would go back a few steps, and pass against it a second time.

She had Pagan eyes, full of nocturnal mysteries, and their light, as it came and went, and came again, was partially hampered by their oppressive lids and lashes; and of these the under lid was much fuller than it usually is with English women. This enabled her to indulge in reverie without seeming to do so: she might have been believed capable of sleeping without closing them up. Assuming that the souls of men and women were visible essences, you could fancy the colour of Eustacia's soul to be flame-like. The sparks from it that rose into her dark pupils gave the same impression.

The Return of the Native was published in 1878, five years after Pater's *Renaissance,* and Walter Pater's visions of Botticelli's Venus and of Leonardo's Mona Lisa clearly influence Hardy's description of his magnetic Eustacia, another fatal woman of the High Decadence, portrayed with a sado-masochistic flavoring. Hardy, perhaps involuntarily, alludes to a memorable sentence of the "Conclusion" to *The Renaissance:*

This at least of flame-like our life has, that it is but the concurrence, renewed from moment to moment, of forces parting sooner or later on their ways.

A heroine with a flame-like soul is bound to destroy herself, and Hardy's ambivalence seems to me purely defensive. Hardy rather liked the inscrutable Pater when they met, and their affinities—aside from temperament—were considerable. We do not ordinarily think of Hardy's Wessex as an aesthetic realm, but what else is it? Pater's conception of tragedy is close to Hardy's: both indirectly descend from Hegel's idea that the genre must feature a conflict between right and right. But Hegel was not an impressionist, and both Pater and Hardy tend to be, as is their common descendent Virginia Woolf.

Yeats, very much in Pater's tradition, said that: "We begin to live when we conceive of life as tragedy." Hardy would not have remarked that, but he believed it, and exemplifies it in his novels. *The Mayor of Casterbridge, Tess of the d'Urbervilles,* and *Jude the Obscure* are novelistic tragedies, closer to Shakespeare than to George Eliot. Tess in particular has something of the universal appeal of Shakespearean tragedy, though the sado-masochistic gratification of the audience/readership is again an equivocal element in Hardy's aesthetic power. And yet who would have it otherwise? *Tess* is the most beautiful of Hardy's pastoral visions, and the tragic Tess is the most disturbing of all his heroines, because she is the most desirable. ❁

Biography of
Thomas Hardy

Thomas Hardy was born on June 2, 1840, in Upper Bockhampton, an area of southwest England that he was to make the "Wessex" of his novels. At that time, Upper Bockhampton was relatively untouched by the social changes and industrialization that were transforming other parts of England. The vast railway system that had been spreading its network across the country in the 1820s and 1830s would not reach Dorset county until 1847. A small but important agricultural center for the surrounding region, Dorset maintained its folk traditions, and those traditions play a vital role in each of the novels discussed here. However, these very same traditions were, at the same time, being challenged by the encroaching forces of an increasingly mechanized world. It is against this background of agricultural labor and such ancient monuments as Stonehenge, that Hardy's characters try to find reprieve. Indeed, they oftentimes seek to find hope and salvation by adhering to the time-tested rhythms of a pastoral labor and rural celebration. However, the men and women in Hardy's novels are not in complete control of their fate but, rather, subject to the mercy of indifferent forces that dictate their behavior and their relationship with others. Nevertheless, outside forces notwithstanding, fate is not a wholly external force and characters are driven by the demands of their own nature as much as by anything from outside them.

Both his father and grandfather, alike named Thomas Hardy, were stonemasons. His mother, Jemima Hand, was an unusually well-read woman, fond of reciting ballads. Hardy later described her as possessing a "wonderful vitality," but instilled with the ancient pessimism of the rural poor. Before he started school, young Thomas Hardy had learned to play the violin and was already fond of music and dance. Hardy's formal education lasted for about eight years in local schools, first, in 1848, at a school in the nearby village presided over by the childless Mrs. Julia Augusta Martin. It is around this time that Hardy's mother gave him copies of Dryden's *Virgil,* Johnson's *Rasselas,* and Saint-Pierre's *Paul and Virginia*—he also discovered his grandfather's copy of the periodical *A History of the Wars,* which dealt with the wars with Napoleon. Michael Millgate says that it was at his first school that Hardy "suffered the earliest experiences of love [for Mrs. Martin], the slighting of the loved one, and the subsequent guilt which were to recur throughout his life" (*Thomas Hardy: A Biography.*) In 1849, Hardy was transferred to a school in Dorchester, primarily because the headmaster was an excellent teacher of Latin. Hardy became well read in English, French, and Latin, enjoying such works as James Grant's *The Scottish Cavalier* and Shakespeare's tragedies. It was also around this time, that Hardy also observed first-hand some of the peasant folkways such as the Christmas mummers, villagers dancing around a maypole, and a prisoner in the stocks at Puddletown. At Christmas in 1854, he was presented with a book entitled *Scenes & Adverstures at Home and Abroad,* a prize he won for diligence and good behavior.

In 1856, Hardy left school and was apprenticed for the next three years to John Hicks, a Dorchester architect and church-restorer, for whom his father had worked. Hicks was a genial and well-educated man in his forties, from whom Hardy received instruction in "architectural drawing and surveying." During these days there was an enthusiastic demand for "medievalism" and religious revivalism, a type of restoration work with which Hicks was primarily engaged. Hardy would later write in "Memories of Church Restoration," that what he most lamented was the interruption of ancient traditions, a feeling that is evidenced throughout his literary works.

Lacking confidence in his knowledge of Latin and his scant knowledge of Greek, Hardy felt he was ill-prepared for university admission. As a result of an acute awareness of these deficiencies, Hardy determined to embark on a rigorous program of self-education. He continued to study Latin and began learning Greek, with much of his reading taking place between five and eight in the morning. It was also at this time that he enjoyed the privilege of meeting his neighbor Mr. William Barnes, a Dorchester schoolmaster and dialect poet of distinction. Then on August 9 Hardy witnessed the execution of Martha Brown for the murder of her husband. It was to leave a lasting impression in his mind and no doubt contributed to the final scene in *Tess of the d'Urbervilles.*

From 1858 to 1861, Hardy began writing poetry, among them "Domicilium," the earliest of his poems to be preserved. He was now assisted in Greek by Horace Moule, eight years his senior and the son of a prominent minister. Because of his inability to pass mathematics, Moule left both Oxford and Cambridge without a degree.

Nevertheless, he managed to win the Hulsean Prize at Cambridge for his work on *Christian Oratory.* That work was published in 1859. He would remain a close friend of Hardy, offering advice and assistance in promoting his protégé's literary career. It has been acknowledged by scholars that Moule did influence Hardy's thinking on modern topics and that Hardy followed the *Saturday Review* for which Moule wrote—particularly on issues concerning the controversy between science and Christian orthodoxy. Moule's suicide in 1873 would have a profound effect on Hardy.

Throughout his life, Thomas Hardy would retain a wide-ranging intellectual curiosity. In the spring of 1863 he heard Dickens lecture and in September 1864 he went to the London School of Phrenology to have his head read by the proprietor. Like many other intellectuals of the time, Hardy would undergo a crisis of faith, precipitated by, among other things, his reading Darwin's *Origin of Species,* of which he counted himself as among the earliest readers. Furthering this crisis of faith was the controversial theological symposium, *Essays and Reviews* (1860), which caused Hardy to abandon the Christianity of his childhood.

On April 17, 1862, his apprenticeship with Hicks now over, the twenty-one year old Thomas Hardy set out for London, which, at this time, was a center of an unprecedented urban growth. He immediately found employment there with Arthur Blomfield, who happened to be in need of a "young Gothic draughtsman" to assist in the restoration and design of churches and rectory-houses. According to Millgate, "his attraction to the Church seems always to have depended not so much upon intellectual conviction as upon the emotion appeal of its rituals and, later, upon its perceived possibilities as an avenue of social and especially educational advancement." Nevertheless, as his literary work demonstrates, he retained a thorough knowledge of the Bible and an interest in church architecture. From 1862 to 1867, Hardy treasured the many glimpses he captured of the customs, manners, and way of life—all of which were quickly disappearing. During this period, he spent his leisure time reading a great deal of Shakespeare from a ten-volume edition he had purchased. In addition to his reading Shakespeare, he read various works that would later serve as a model for argumentative prose.

Hardy also demonstrated a love of music, an interest he shared with Blomfield. He again took up the violin while, at the same time, methodically reading the *Old Testament* and all of the major poets, including Spenser, Shakespeare, Burns, Byron, Wordsworth, Tennyson, William Barnes, and Swinburne whose *Poems and Ballads* (1866) Hardy was particularly enamored of.

Hardy began writing poetry during the period of 1865–1867, which he submitted to the magazines. However, this first attempt at poetry was a failure and resulted in his destroying many of the poems; which he considered to be of the poorest quality. Nevertheless, as F. B. Pinion remarks, many of these poems "are remarkable in their relentless confrontation of the truth, however chilling. Love deceives; beauty is subject to the ravages of time; and chance and indifference rule the universe." (*A Hardy Companion*) These deeply felt convictions were borne of his readings in science where concepts of the universe and the individual's importance within this cosmic scheme were changing. Similarly, science was having a profound impact on Hardy's religious beliefs, such that the universe was now seen as being neutral and indifferent to the plight of man.

The reality of the publishing industry at the time was that fiction was a far more marketable and lucrative genre than poetry and thus marked Hardy's entrance into writing fiction. His first novel was *The Poor Man and the Lady,* a social satire that remained unpublished, having been rejected by the publishers in 1868 on the recommendation of George Meredith. Nevertheless, despite his criticism, Meredith advised Hardy to continue writing, the result of which advice was *Desperate Remedies,* published anonymously in 1871. Published in the conventional and expensive three-volume form, it was a novel similar to the very popular sensational novels of Wilkie Collins and others, but its reception was very unenthusiastic. The *Athenaeum* review of April 1871 described it as "an unpleasant story" while the *Spectator* review, also in April of 1871, called it "disagreeable, and not striking in any way," while lauding Hardy's skill in depicting rural life.

The following year saw Hardy's career as a novelist successfully launched with the publication of *Under the Greenwood Tree* in 1872. His shortest novel quickly became a classic. *Under the Greenwood Tree* is a love story that ends with the marriage of the heroine, Fancy Day, to the unassuming Dick Dewey. It is also a story of the changing social conditions under which the old ways of the village lose ground to mechanical interventions. Hardy's friend, Horace

Moule, an accomplished classical scholar and writer on the contemporary debate between science and Christian orthodoxy, praised the work. Moule described it as "the best prose idyll we have seen for a long while past." Interestingly, Moule's critique points out the influence of George Eliot's early work in addition to *Silas Marner*. Hardy's subtitle to this work, A *Rural Painting of the Dutch School,* is a phrase to be found in Eliot's *Adam Bede.* Hardy's newfound success would soon allow him to give up his architectural work and embark on a series of novels that would end with *Jude the Obscure* in 1895 when the hostile reception of this novel sent him back to poetry.

In 1870, during his travel to St. Juliot on the coast of Cornwall for architectural business, Hardy began a long courtship with Emma Lavinia Gifford, the sister-in-law of the local clergyman. Emma Lavinia, who came from a middle class family and whose uncle was an archdeacon, was of a higher social status than Hardy. Despite opposition from both of their families, Hardy and Gifford married on September 17, 1874. Hardy's earning capacity increased with the success of *Far from the Madding Crowd* thus enabling him to devote his full energies to his writing. The couple's wedding, which was held in London and at which no member of his own family was in attendance, took place while *Far from the Madding Crowd* was serialized in the *Cornhill.* Nevertheless, the marriage which began happily would later cause great heartache and bitterness. Although supportive of Hardy's literary career, Emma Lavinia was obsessed with both her social superiority and her own writing talents. In fact, she was very much opposed to the subject matter of *Jude the Obscure* and tried to prevent its publication.

During this busy and fruitful time of 1871, Hardy was also planning his next novel, *A Pair of Blue Eyes.* This story focused on social differences and their impact on love relationships. The heroine, Elfride Swancourt, is loved by two men—Stephen Smith, "a rural builder's son" and Henry Knight, an urbane intellectual. But perhaps even more significant was the novel's glimpse into the Victorian awareness of scientific discoveries as well as the Victorian understanding of concepts of space and time. One particular scene demonstrates the immensity of geological time with the corresponding diminution of human life. While Henry Knight is hanging from a cliff and about to fall to his death, he observes "an imbedded fossil. . . . It was one of the early crustaceans called Trilobites. Separated by millions of years in their lives, Knight and this underling seem to have met in their place of death." *A Pair of Blue Eyes* contains some important autobiographical features as well, including Henry Knight's resemblance to Horace Moule. Prior to its final publication in 1873, *A Pair of Blue Eyes* was serialized in the periodical *Tinsleys' Magazine.* This serialization was to set a precedent whereby all of Hardy's subsequent novels would make their initial appearance as episodes in a periodical. 1873 also marked the year of Moule's suicide. Having served Hardy as mentor and friend, this tragedy deeply affected Hardy. Robert Gittings marks Moule's death as Hardy's transformation into a "a fully tragic artist, an expounder of man's true miseries."

Hardy's success as a novelist continued to mount with the publication of *The Hand of Ethelberta* in 1876, *The Return of the Native* in 1878 and a minor novel, *The Trumpet-Major,* in 1880. By this time, Hardy had established himself in a London suburb where he was near the literary circles of the day. He dined out regularly, often met celebrities, and took occasional vacations on the Continent, yet by 1880 the Hardys still had no permanent home. It was here that he also formed such lasting friendships as the one he had with London writer and critic Edmund Gosse whom he had met at the Savile Club. However, 1880 also marked a significant setback for Hardy when he became seriously ill with an internal hemorrhage. He remained in bed for several months, all the while dictating his novel, *A Laodicean,* to Emma. The least successful of his novels, its hero is an architect and the heroine an heiress. The narrative is replete with the trappings of Victorian melodrama and intrigue. Upon his recovery in the Spring of 1881, he and his wife set out to find a house in Hardy's native county of Dorset and in 1882 he published his third minor novel, *Two on a Tower.* Here, the hero is a young astronomer, Swithin St. Cleeve, romantically involved with a high-born woman, Lady Constantine, set amidst the background of "the stellar universe." After settling down in Wimborne Minster in 1881, Hardy put down some roots in Dorset by joining such groups as the Dorset Natual History and Antiquarian Field Club. He also spent a considerable amount of time in London with literary personalities in clubs, salons, and dinner parties. Nevertheless, Hardy's financial position was strong and he set to building a house according to his own design outside Dorchester. The house would be called Max Gate (after Henry Mack, a former toll-gate keeper of the neighborhood) and the couple took up residence in June 1885. Hardy would live there for the rest of his life.

This move to Dorchester was to influence Hardy's creative life and influenced the first novel he wrote after returning to Dorchester, *The Mayor of Casterbridge,* which he began writing in 1884 and completed in April 1885. *The Mayor of Casterbridge,* which takes place around mid-century, therefore going back a generation before the date of composition, is suffused with a profound sense of loss. It depicts the destruction of a way of life by fate, historical and social circumstances, and the misguided judgment of certain characters. Though professional reviewers did not appreciate the novel, George Gissing, Robert Louis Stevenson, and Gerard Manley Hopkins had praise for *The Mayor of Casterbridge.*

In November 1885, Hardy began *The Woodlanders* with the new burst of energy that characterized his return to his native Dorset. A novel which was not well received by some Victorian reviewers, *The Woodlanders* had readers uncomfortable with Hardy's insistence on taking up highly controversial moral and social issues. On the other hand, the *Athenaeum* found the novel to be "simply perfect." This was followed by, among other works, *Tess of the d'Urbervilles* in 1891 and an essay, "Candour in English Fiction," published in the *New Review* in January 1890. The "Candour" essay focuses on the "fearful price" that a principled artist pays for "the privilege of writing in the English language," due to the pressures exerted by editors and librarians and the existence of the "young person" standard. For Hardy, life is "a physiological fact" and "its honest portrayal must be largely concerned with, for one thing, the relations of the sexes." Finally, following the controversy of *Jude the Obscure,* Hardy ceased writing novels.

From this time forward in the last years of the nineteenth century, Hardy spent his time and energy writing and publishing verse, with his first volume of poetry, *Wessex Poems,* appearing in 1898. The poems contain many of Hardy's characteristic attitudes and beliefs, a number of them being anecdotes illustrating the perversity of fate and the ironies of coincidence. Long impatient with the constraints of serialized fiction and by now having become rich from the success of his novels, Hardy continued to write poetry and short stories. He also wrote an epic-drama of the Napoleonic Wars, *The Dynasts,* which came out in three parts between 1903 and 1908. While spending more and more time at Max Gate, he received a steady stream of visitors, including the Prince of Wales. Though he was offered a knighthood, he declined. In 1910, however, he did accept the Order of Merit, the highest honor that can be paid an English author. Fifteen months following the death of his first wife, Emma Hardy, on November 27, 1912, he married Florence Emily Dugdale, a teacher approximately forty years his junior. Nevertheless, many of his poems provide a powerful expression to his sense of loss with the death of Emma Hardy. On January 11, 1928, Hardy died at Max Gate at the age of eighty-seven. ✿

Plot Summary of
Far from the Madding Crowd

Published in 1874 and serialized in the *Cornhill* magazine from January–December 1874, *Far from the Madding Crowd* is the Wessex novel with which Hardy attained general popularity. Hardy is here very interested in conveying emotional feelings. Detailed pictorial and scenic representations are made to reflect emotional responses to situations. While admiring the "poetry" in this novel, Leslie Stephen was concerned about the propriety of the scandalous story of Fanny Robin and the length of the sheering scene for the serial magazine readership. During the time in which he was writing Tess, Hardy was coping with the traumatic event of Moule's suicide and some of that anguish appears as a variation on the pastoral theme; which conventionally does not contain themes of emotional disturbance and murder.

   Chapter 1 introduces Farmer Oak (Gabriel), the protagonist of the novel, a twenty-eight year old farmer. He is not handsome, his "features adher[ing] throughout their form so exactly to the middle line between the beauty of St. John and the ugliness of Judas Iscariot . . . that not a single lineament could be selected and called worthy either of distinction or notoriety." Yet, as his name suggests, he is solid in character and demeanor and, accordingly he is well respected by all of his village neighbors. Gabriel Oak is also in complete harmony with nature, demonstrating his love and reverence for the animals in his care, and a respect for nature, here his native Norcombe Hill. "Being a man not without a frequent consciousness that there was some charm in this life he led . . . looking at the sky as a useful instrument . . . an appreciative spirit, as a work of art superlatively beautiful." Indeed, the description of Norcombe Hill evokes the sense that it is a force to be reckoned with and a presence that will participate in the unfolding story. While walking, Gabriel Oak sees a gaily-painted wagon coming towards him and we soon find out that a very vain and beautiful young woman is gazing at her reflection in a mirror. "She simply observed herself as a fair product of Nature in the feminine kind." As it turns out, this woman is the one whom Gabriel will later pursue and, eventually, marry. At the turnpike-gate, an argument ensues as the young woman refuses to pay the gatekeeper an extra two pence. Gabriel Oak puts an end to it by paying the two pence to the gatekeeper himself—a gesture the young woman does not appreciate. Though she is beautiful, Farmer Oak recognizes that her's is not an innocent beauty. **Chapter 2** continues to portray the idyllic beauty of this pastoral setting, "the panoramic glide of the stars past earthly objects," and Gabriel's participation in it. While inside his simple hut, playing a flute, Farmer Oak hears the bleating of a lamb and rushes outside to carry the lamb back to its mother.

In **Chapter 3,** Gabriel finds the young woman's hat lying in a ditch and soon sees her riding towards Tewnell Mill. When he finally encounters her and tells her of his infatuation, she is unimpressed. A little further on, while keeping his usual watch for the young woman, he falls asleep only to awaken on her lap as she tries to revive him from the smoke within. Though Oak expresses his gratitude to her, she will not allow him to hold her hand. He finally learns that her name is Bathsheba Everdene and that she is staying with her aunt in a nearby cottage. Gabriel decides to propose to Bathsheba, even though she has done nothing to encourage him. He is rebuffed by her aunt, Mrs. Hurst, who explains that Bathsheba is an excellent scholar, trained to be a governess and has had many proposals from suitable young men. For the first time in his life, Oak regrets his humble stature, stating "I'm only an every-day sort of man, and my only chance was in being the first comer. . . ." He takes leave of her aunt while Bathsheba races after him, only to feign interest in him.

Chapter 5 depicts Oak's suffering as the younger and more unruly of his two dogs herds his flock of sheep to the edge a precipice thereby causing the untimely death of some 200 sheep and their unborn lambs. Since he has no insurance for his sheep, Gabriel is forced to sell the remainder of his flock to pay his debts. Two months later, in **Chapter 6,** Gabriel Oak attends a hiring-fair in the town of Casterbridge. He hopes to find employment as a bailiff, but he does not succeed in getting hired. A short time later, while walking across a field, Gabriel notices a wheat rick on fire which threatens to destroy a huge pile of hay stacks nearby. After organizing the other workers and extinguishing the fire, he soon encounters his beloved Bathsheba, the owner of the farm, while his fame in the district is soon widely acclaimed.

In **Chapter 8,** at Warren's Malthouse, a group of rustics is assembled who warmly welcome Gabriel to drink from the "God-forgive-me" cup. Here he learns that Pennyways, a none-too-honest bailiff, manages Bathsheba's farm. One day, Bathsheba found him "creeping down the granary steps with half a bushel of barley." **Chapter 9** begins with a description of Bathsheba Everdene's home, an old mansion-like structure with its walls covered in moss. "By daylight, the bower of Oak's new-found mistress . . . presented itself as a hoary building, of the early stage of Classical Renaissance" a style characteristic of the late sixteenth century, and of a size which indicated it had once been a manorial hall. A visitor is heard knocking on the door, Farmer Boldwood, who has called to inquire regarding the whereabouts of the young servant girl Fanny Robin. Boldwood is a bachelor about forty years in age, very rich and extremely handsome—he leaves immediately upon hearing that there is no news of Fanny. A little further on, in **Chapter 10,** Bathsheba tells the other men about the dismissal of the thieving bailiff and her determination to manage her farm by herself. She appoints Cainy Ball as under-shepherd, a young man whose name was a mistake on his mother's part. "[H]is poor mother, not being a Scripture-read woman, made a mistake at his christening. Thinking it 'twas Abel killed Cain." In the meantime William Smallbury brings news that Fanny has run away in search of Sergeant Troy, who is less than enthused to see her. When asked what arrangements he has made for their marriage, his responses always turn to trivial excuses for having acted. Fanny leaves with his promise to see her the next day at Mrs. Twill's.

In **Chapter 12,** Bathsheba makes her first appearance as farm-manager in the corn market at Casterbridge and soon realizes that she must make a concerted effort to present herself as confident. Nevertheless, despite her demeanor, there is one farmer who remains unimpressed—Mr. Boldwood. "Bathseba was convinced that this unmoved person was not a married man." According to Liddy, he has suffered a terrible disappointment in love as a younger man. We are also told that Boldwood, a tenant farmer, is considered to be a member of the landed gentry, and that he leads a peaceful and unremarkable life in accordance with his calm temperament. It is, therefore, no surprise (**Chapter 13**) that Liddy encourages Bathsheba to send him an anonymous Valentine's Day card, on which is inscribed "'The rose is red, / The violet blue, / Carnation's sweet, / And so are you." Nevertheless, the valentine greeting is insincere, a mere game to Bathsheba. "'It just suits itself to a chubby-faced child like him.'"

When the scene shifts to the Malthouse (**Chapter 15**), we find Gabriel coming to Bathsheba's defense in response to the condemnation of the other labourers, threatening to respond to anyone who sets about "prophesying bad of our mistress," and Boldwood reappearing to deliver a letter from Fanny Robin. Fanny has written to Gabriel to thank him for his kindness. Delivering the letter has also provided Boldwood with the opportunity to show the Valentine Card to Gabriel with the hope that the latter can identify the signature. Gabriel immediately recognizes it to be that of Bathsheba Everdene.

In the meantime, while these various encounters between Bathsheba and Boldwood are taking place, another ancillary drama has been unfolding between a soldier, Sergeant Troy, and a poor orphaned servant girl, Fanny Robin. **Chapter 16** opens with a morning church service on All Saints' day and a soldier, in uniform, marching up the aisle, waiting for his absent and pregnant bride, Fanny Robin. The soldier is quite noticeably embarrassed as he stands rigid, while the congregation is buzzing away at the bride's abandonment. After waiting half an hour, the soldier leaves the church, whereupon he soon meets Fanny who explains her delay. "The expression of her face, which had been one of intense anxiety, sank at the sight of his nearly to terror." It seems that she has gone to All Souls' Church by mistake, but the soldier is feeling far too humiliated and, thus dismisses her plea for forgiveness. He quickly leaves her stranded, departing with a ironic remark that he did not know when their wedding would take place.

Chapter 19 begins with Boldwood calling again on Bathsheba. Indeed, he has formed a highly idealized image of her. "The great aids to idealization in love were present here: occasional observation of her from a distance, and the absence of social intercourse with her—visual familiarity, oral strangeness." In a word, Boldwood is smitten and, when he finally proposes marriage, Bathsheba responds that she does not love him. Despite Boldwood's entreaty, Bathsheba can only apologize for misleading him with her anonymous card, stating that "'it was a wanton thing which no woman with any self-respect should have done.'" But Boldwood remains steadfast, obsessed with winning her, as Bathsheba considers his proposal as socially advantageous. In truth, Bathsheba loves her independence and her new position while Gabriel Oak remains silently in love with her, though he soon has an opportunity to prove himself to her.

A crisis develops in **Chapter 21,** when Bathsheba's sheep wander to a clover field and fall ill. Laban Tall advises her to summon Gabriel Oak as the only person who can save them. Though her pride has previously been wounded by the forthright Mr. Oak, who has no qualms in criticizing her vanity, the sight of the dead and the dying sheep causes her to dismiss her pride, "[s]woln with wind and the rank mist they drew." Gabriel comes to her aid and saves the sheep by performing a minor surgical procedure on each of them. He is also now confident of her feelings for him and, thus, agrees to stay on the farm. During the shearing (**Chapter 22**), Boldwood appears in order to talk to Bathseba, while Gabriel observes their interaction, and proceeds to get quite upset when the two go off together. "Gabriel sheared on, constrained and sad." Boldwood has come with the intention of proposing marriage, but Bathsheba will stall for time. Indeed, Gabriel is so upset that he begins to work carelessly, all the while thinking about Bathsheba's hint that he would be made the bailiff. Gabriel is eager for the job, as it would afford him the opportunity to work closely with her. **Chapter 23** begins with a festive occasion, the shearing supper, with Bathsheba seated at the head of the table. She has asked Gabriel to sit at the bottom of the table so that he may act as host to the villagers. However, when Boldwood arrives, Gabriel is asked to relinquish his seat. The villagers continue to celebrate with songs and poetry recitations. Jacob Smallbury restores peace by starting a ballad which repeats over and over, "'I've lost my love, and I care not,'" while Bathsheba sings a song about a soldier and his bride to the tune of Gabriel's flute. "Subsequent events caused one of the verse to be remembered for many months, and even years, by more than one of those who were gathered there—'For his bried a solider sought her, / And a winning tongue had he.'"

In **Chapter 24,** Bathsheba encounters Sergeant Troy one evening while on her way to inspect the farm grounds. While trying to make her way back home through a path of fir trees, Bathsheba hears a man's voice stating that their clothes have become entangled. Though she tries to resist helping him, the sergeant sets to disentangling them, all the while taking his time so that he may look at her. Shortly thereafter, when she returns home, Liddy tells Bathsheba about Troy's bad reputation and **Chapter 25** provides a character sketch of the young soldier. He is impulsive, never caring for the past or worried about the future and his behavior towards women is dishonorable. As he is well-educated, he is skilled in making flattering speeches. "He spoke fluently and unceasingly. He could in this way be one thing and seem another; for instance he could speak of love and think of dinner; call on the husband to look at the wife; be eager to pay and intend to owe." Bathsheba again encounters Troy (**Chapter 26**) and is vulnerable to his charms as he claims to have fallen in love with her at first sight. He even goes so far as to present her with a gold watch, a family heirloom belonging to the Earls of Severn. The two part company, agreeing to meet again. Later in June (**Chapter 27**), a day after meeting with Troy, Bathsheba decides to hive the bees herself when Troy reappears to lend assistance. At eight o'clock that evening, Bathsheba sets out to meet Troy (**Chapter 28**). He is waiting with great anticipation for the opportunity to impress her with his sword tricks, and manages to cut a lock of her hair and kisses her as he leaves. Bathsheba is upset, feeling as though she has committed a sin. Nevertheless, she has fallen in love with him against her better judgment. When she seeks out Gabriel's advice, he is very direct about his reservations concerning Troy's unworthiness (**Chapter 29**) while reminding her of her promise to marry Boldwood for the sake of her reputation. She and Gabriel argue about Troy as Bathsheba tells him to leave the farm. Indeed, Bathsheba's infatuation with Troy is a great source of contention for others, especially Boldwood who curses the young soldier in the face of Bathsheba's rejection. And in **Chapter 32**, Bathsheba sets out to find Troy, deliberately deceiving herself that Troy will encourage her to stay away from him. "Was Bathsheba altogether blind to the obvious fact that the support of a lover's arms is not of a kind best calculated to assist a resolve to renounce him?" And Gabriel Oak, on hearing of Bathsheba's meeting with Troy, is now convinced that she will never love him.

Nevertheless, Gabriel will once again rescue a desperate situation. "'I will help to my last effort the woman I have loved so dearly.'" It is now the end of August, and Troy is married to Bathsheba and in charge of her farm, where he is giving a festive harvest supper (**Chapter 36**). At the same time, Gabriel observes a bad storm brewing with eight unprotected ricks in the yard. When Troy foolishly refuses to listen to Gabriel regarding the imminent disaster, Gabriel becomes resolute that he must act alone. Though he asks to speak with Troy, the latter foolishly refuses. Since Gabriel, a laborer, cannot walk up to Troy himself, he again sends a message that heavy rain will ruin the harvest, but Troy again ignores his advice, offering brandy to the workers despite Bathsheba's request not to. The messenger returns to

Oak, stating that Troy does not believe it will rain. Not wishing to displease Troy, Oak stays for a while and then departs for home, observing the sheep are terrified by the coming storm. Gabriel determines that he must protect Bathsheba and that he must act alone.

In **Chapter 39,** Bathsheba and Troy encounter the lonely and weakened figure of Fanny Robin, who has been absent for many chapters. Her reappearance in the narrative serves as a harbinger of the disruption to the unhappy marriage of Bathsheba and Troy. In **Chapter 40,** the full weight of the tragic events in Fanny's life finally is felt as she crawls along the highway with the help of a compassionate dog. "[H]e was the ideal embodiment of canine greatness. . . . Darkness endows the small and ordinary ones among mankind with poetical power, and even the suffering woman threw her idea into figure." Fanny finally succumbs as we learn from Joseph Poorgrass in **Chapter 41.** Even more tragically, Fanny dies with her newborn baby in her arms. Bathsheba makes the funeral arrangements. It is only a short time before Bathsheba makes the anguished discovery that Fanny's lover is none other than her husband Troy. Indeed, after the coffin is brought into her house (**Chapter 43**), Bathesheba opens the lid to confirm her suspicions and gazes in shock at the sight of Fanny and her baby. Meanwhile, though Troy had previously tried to erase any possible evidence of his connection with Fanny Robin, he is forced to admit the truth when he returns to the open coffin. It is at this time that Bathsheba now receives the worst blow of all as Troy tells her that Fanny means far more to him than Bathsheba ever will. "If Satan had not tempted me with that face of yours, and those cursed coquetries, I should have married her." Haunted by his culpability and estranged from Bathsheba, Troy leaves Weatherbury. The first Saturday after Troy's departure (**Chapter 48**) Bathsheba visits the Casterbridge market where she learns that Troy has drowned at sea. Though she tries to deny the truth to herself, there is evidence in the form of a newspaper story based on the alleged eyewitness account of a young physician and the return of Troy's watch and clothing.

Chapter 49 resumes the narrative a full year later and Gabriel Oak is now the official bailiff of Bathsheba's farm. Indeed, Gabriel's rising fortune is the subject of village gossip and he is wrongly accused of putting on airs. As Susan Tall observes, "'[w]hen I see people strut enough to be cut up into bantam cocks, I stand dormant with wonder, and says no more!'" At the same time, with Troy's disappearance,

Boldwood assumes that there is no legal obstacle to prevent him from proposing to Bathsheba, though he will ultimately be rejected. Furthermore, unbeknownst to everyone, we learn that Troy has been working in America all this time (**Chapter 50**). Upon his return, he intends to evade Bathsheba by joining a traveling circus. But, as fate would have it, the circus visits Greenhill for the annual sheep fair and Bathsheba is there. Though he initially tries to conceal his identity, he is discovered by Pennyways and flees.

Chapter 52 finds Boldwood hosting a Christmas party with the expectation that he will finally receive the long-awaited answer of Bathsheba consenting to marry him. Though Gabriel Oak tries to suggest that he should not get his hopes up, Boldwood refuses to heed his advice and instead puts a diamond ring his pocket. Meanwhile, Troy is now seated at a tavern in Casterbridge with Pennyways, who tells him of Boldwood's party and Bathsheba's attendance. Troy decides to disguise himself at the party in order to observe Bathsheba, donning a "a heavy grey overcoat of Noachian [biblical] cut, with cape and high collar, the latter being erect and rigid, like a girdling wall." But four of Boldwood's men have already spotted him through the window of the tavern (**Chapter 53**). Furthermore, when Troy arrives at the party, Bathsheba recognizes him, and when he tries to force Bathsheba to leave the party with him, Boldwood takes out a gun and shoots him.

Shortly thereafter, Boldwood confesses his murder by surrendering at the Casterbridge jail (**Chapter 54**). Gabriel soon arrives at the party to find the guests horrified and Bathsheba holding the dead body of Troy in her arms. For her part, Bathsheba blames herself for the terrible tragedy. Some eight months following Troy's murder, Bathsheba is consigned to a very lonely existence. When Gabriel announces that he is leaving for California, Bathsheba suggests that she might be willing to marry him (**Chapter 56**). Oak is very surprised as he had long since given up all hope of marrying her. Soon after, Bathsheba and Gabriel are married one misty morning before the parson (**Chapter 57**). The village folk gather outside her parlor to celebrate their happiness and goodwill towards the newly-weds. "Just as Bathsheba was pouring out a cup of tea, their ears were greeted by the firing of a cannon, followed by what seemed like a tremendous blowing of trumpets, in the front of the house." ✸

List of Characters in
Far from the Madding Crowd

Gabriel Oak – The novel's hero, Gabriel Oak is a farmer, a shepherd, and a bailiff, marked by humble and honest ways, possessing exceptional skill with animals and farming, and an unparalleled loyalty. He fulfills many roles, first as Bathsheba's first suitor, then as bailiff on her farm and, finally, her husband at the very end of the novel. He is in complete harmony with the natural world and, as a quiet observer throughout most of the novel, is always there to save Bathsheba and others from the consequences of their bad judgment.

Bathsheba Everdene – The beautiful and vain young woman who must choose among three very different suitors. At the beginning of the novel, she is penniless, but she quickly inherits and manages a farm in Weatherbury. Her behavior is usually rash and impulsive.

Sergeant Francis (Frank) Troy – Troy is a less responsible male equivalent of Bathsheba. He is handsome, vain, and young—though capable of love. Early in the novel he is involved with Fanny Robin and gets her pregnant. At first, he plans to marry her, but when they miscommunicate about which church to meet in, he angrily refuses to marry her. Instead, he marries the rich and beautiful Bathsheba. However, when Fanny dies of poverty and exhaustion later in the novel with his child in her arms, he is consumed with inconsolable grief.

William Boldwood – Another of Bathsheba's suitors and the owner of a nearby farm. As his name suggests, Boldwood is somewhat rigid and reserved. Unable to fall in love again until Bathsheba sends him a valentine on a whim, he develops powerful feelings for her, and refuses to give up the pursuit. Ultimately, he shoots Bathsheba's husband Troy at a Christmas party and is sentenced to life in prison.

Fanny Robin – A young, orphaned servant girl at the farm. She attempts to marry Sergeant Troy, and finally dies having already given birth to Troy's child.

Liddy Smallbury – Bathsheba's maid and confidant, of about the same age as Bathsheba.

Jan Coggan – Farm laborer and friend to Gabriel Oak.

Joseph Poorgrass – A shy, timid farm laborer who blushes easily, Poorgrass carries Fanny's coffin from Casterbridge back to the farm for burial.

Cainy Ball – A young boy who works as Gabriel Oak's assistant shepherd on the Everdene farm.

Pennyways – The bailiff on Bathsheba's farm who is caught stealing grain and dismissed. He disappears for most of the novel until he recognizes Troy at Greenhill Fair and helps Troy surprise Bathsheba at Boldwood's Christmas party. ❀

Critical Views on
Far from the Madding Crowd

HOWARD BABB ON SETTING AND THEME

[Howard Babb is the author of *Jane Austen's Novels: The Fabric of Dialogue* (1962) and the editor of *Essays in Stylistic Analysis* (1972). In the excerpt below from his article, "Setting and Theme in *Far from the Madding Crowd*," Babb discusses some of the relationships Hardy creates between natural setting and theme.]

Even casual readers of Thomas Hardy soon begin to sense that in his fiction the customary setting, the natural world, operates a good deal more forcefully than as sheer backdrop to the narrative. And the power of his settings is a commonplace among Hardy's critics, most of whom find the natural background functioning symbolically at moments, though one of them speaks instead of a metaphoric dimension.[1] ⟨. . .⟩ What I want chiefly to bring out in the following pages is both the number and variety of relationships that Hardy creates between setting and theme here: a host of interconnections that serves—along with the story's other structures, some of which I shall be glancing at—to saturate *Far from the Madding Crowd* with its theme. And I shall be suggesting incidentally that the novel's saturation with its theme helps to explain how we come to terms—if indeed we do—with several scenes of more or less questionable plausibility in which the natural setting plays a dominant part.

At bottom, Hardy's story juxtaposes two different worlds or modes of being, the natural against the civilized, and it insists on the superiority of the former by identifying the natural as strong, enduring, self-contained, slow to change, sympathetic, while associating the civilized with weakness, facility, modernity, self-centeredness. We are perhaps alerted for this theme by the title itself of the novel, which evokes the contrast in Gray's "Elegy" between rural and urban values. But in any case, Hardy's juxtaposition of the natural and the civilized is reflected in even the barest outline of *Far from the Madding Crowd*'s narrative. The first section of the story hinges on the unsuccessful marriage proposal made by Gabriel Oak—the simple, modest shepherd—to the self-assured and somewhat flighty

Bathsheba Everdene; she turns him down mainly because she does not love him, to be sure, but also because she has her sights set on a way of life above, somehow more refined than, what he can offer her. By the end of the novel, however, she has learned through her sufferings on account of Boldwood and Troy how to value Gabriel, so Oak's patient love is rewarded at last. Between these opening and closing movements of the story, its foreground is largely given over to the entanglement of Bathsheba with Gabriel's two rivals for her heart. The first to present himself is the gentlemanly Boldwood, whose composure is so shattered by Bathsheba's valentine that he begins hounding her mercilessly to marry him. Then comes the fashionable Troy, who overwhelms Bathsheba with flattery, quickly marries her, tires of her almost as fast, and drifts away after quarreling with her over the dead Fanny Robin, a girl whom Troy seduced before meeting Bathsheba. Finally Boldwood steps forward again, now spurred by the assumption that Troy is dead to press Bathsheba more relentlessly than ever for a promise of marriage, only to have his fantasy exploded by the return of Troy, whom he shoots down in a burst of passion. Every so often during these romantic conflicts and maneuverings, Gabriel Oak will move to the front of the stage, perhaps to give Bathsheba some moral counsel, or to save her sheep, or to protect her grain during the storm. But for the most part he remains in the middle distance, allied with the processes of nature through performing the ordinary tasks of the farmer or shepherd, his feet firmly planted in the natural world. The most general impression created by the narrative, then, is of a running contrast between dignified naturalness and the feverish pursuit of selfish ends.

Whatever the local action that Hardy places in the foreground, he manages to keep us constantly aware of the natural world in the novel. Four characteristics of that world as it is revealed throughout Hardy's fiction have been admirably set forth by John Holloway: "Nature is an organic living whole," with all its parts having "a life and personality of their own"; "it is unified on a great scale through both time and space"; "it is exceedingly complex," with "details that are sometimes even quaint or bizarre"; "these heterogeneous things are integrated, however obscurely, into a system of rigid and undeviating law."[2] ⟨. . .⟩ But the natural world in this novel seems endowed with a fifth attribute as well, one that may surprise the reader of Hardy's other fiction. For in *Far from the Madding Crowd* nature is frequently represented as at least a sympathetic force, sometimes even as a moral agent—an assertion that I shall depend upon details cited later to bear out.

Even if the claim about a fifth attribute should prove tenuous, there can be no questioning the fact that again and again in this story Hardy uses his position as omniscient author to set the natural world and the civilized explicitly against each other in such a way that we have no doubt about which we are to prefer. Almost at the beginning of the novel, for instance, after he has developed so compelling a sense of nature's majesty in describing Norcombe Hill, the night sky, and the "almost . . . palpable movement" of the earth, Hardy remarks that this vivid experiencing of the universe is possible only when one has "first expanded with a sense of difference from the mass of civilized mankind, who are dreamwrapt and disregardful of all such [natural] proceedings at this time" (pp. 9–10).[3]

1. Carol R. Andersen, "Time, Space, and Perspective in Thomas Hardy," *Nineteenth-Century Fiction*, 9 (1954), 192–208. The critic feels that in the case of Hardy "we must take all the ordinary elements of the novel (landscape, characters, plot) and accept them as metaphorical equivalents of the theme" (p. 195), and later speaks of Hardy's "backgrounds" as "something more than a mere setting of scene. It appears to be the pathetic fallacy driven to such an extreme that it is no longer a fallacy but an artistic integer" (p. 203). These sentences convey an impression of Hardy's settings that seems to me much like my own, but the essay concentrates on metaphors of "time" and "space" in the novels.

2. *The Victorian Sage* (London, 1953), p. 252.

3. My Hardy quotations are from Harper's Anniversary Edition of *Far from the Madding Crowd* (New York and London, 1920).

—Howard Babb, "Setting and Theme in *Far from the Madding Crowd*," *ELH* 30, no. 2 (June 1963): pp. 147–49.

Richard C. Carpenter on Mirror Imagery

[Richard C. Carpenter is the author of *Thomas Hardy* (1964). In the excerpt below from his article, "The Mirror and the Sword: Imagery in *Far from the Madding Crowd*," Carpenter discusses Hardy's use of mirror imagery to deepen the reader's emotional and conceptual response.]

⟨. . .⟩ Not until *Far From the Madding Crowd,* the first of the major novels, was Hardy to achieve an integrated design such as we find in *Tess of the d'Urbervilles* or *The Mayor of Casterbridge.* One of the reasons why these novels are "major" is precisely that in them Hardy managed to create a fabric of images, repeated and "concatenated" to deepen and make complex the emotional and conceptual significance. The structure of images in *The Return of the Native* is as much superior to that of *Two on a Tower* as are the plot and theme.

To see how this is applicable to *Far From the Madding Crowd,* I wish to take a passage from the early part of the novel and trace out some of the ways in which its images are used as the story moves on. The passage I have in mind comes directly after our introduction to Gabriel Oak, the representative of rural stability and firmness. As he glances casually over the hedge at the side of a road, he sees "an ornamental spring waggon, painted yellow and gaily marked, drawn by two horses, a waggoner walking alongside bearing a whip perpendicularly" (p. 3).[1] The "waggon" is piled high with household furniture and plants, while a "young and attractive woman" sits on the "apex" of the load. The wagoner leaves her for a few minutes, while he goes back to retrieve the tailboard, which has fallen off. She waits "for some time idly in her place" until she looks attentively down at a package wrapped in paper, which she unwraps to reveal a "small swing looking-glass." She gazes at herself in this mirror, then parts her lips and smiles:

> It was a fine morning, and the sun lighted up to a scarlet glow the crimson jacket she wore, and painted a soft lustre upon her bright face and dark hair. The myrtles, geraniums, and cactuses packed around her were fresh and green, and at such a leafless season they invested the whole concern of horses, waggon, furniture, and girl with a peculiar vernal charm. What possessed her to indulge in such a performance in the sight of the sparrows, blackbirds, and unperceived farmer who were alone its spectators,— whether the smile began as a factitious one, to test her capacity in that art,—nobody knows; it ended certainly in a real smile. She blushed at herself, and seeing her reflection blush, blushed the more (p. 5).

Hardy cannot resist, at this stage of his career, commenting wrily on "woman's prescriptive infirmity," but he does not succeed in spoiling the effect of this vivid bit of characterization.

Although this scene is memorable because of its presentational quality—its vivid colors of scarlet, green, and yellow; its visual composition; the contrasts of bright face and dark hair, crimson jacket and green plants, vernal freshness and leafless season, it is also part of a larger context with which it interacts, and individual images are lifted out of it to be employed in many different ways throughout the novel. The imagistic design of *Far From the Madding Crowd*, unlike the straightforward structure of its narrative, is fundamentally musical. A motif, announced in an early scene, reappears time after time, sometimes as a leitmotiv attached to similar situations or characters and gaining in significance because of repetition in an expanding milieu, but more often transposed, inverted, taken up by a different character or situation. For example, when Bathsheba Everdene meets Gabriel Oak in later scene—also a crucial one—several images of this first episode are evident, now transposed and varied. Oak has fallen in love with Bathsheba, been refused, and lost his entire flock of sheep in an accident; while she, without his knowing it, has inherited a prosperous farm from her uncle and is now the owner of a thousand acres. It is night and one of her straw ricks has caught fire. The flames reflect on Gabriel's face as he passes by, with a "rich orange glow." Not a living soul seems to be about, and he watches as an interested spectator only, until the smoke swirling aside shows that a number of grain-ricks are in danger, whereupon he starts to work to quell the fire, several of Bathsheba's workmen coming up to help. When Bathsheba finally arrives, Gabriel is on top of the rick fighting the fire. ⟨...⟩

The mirror is an ambivalent symbol. As we see it in Hawthorne, for example, it shows the inner truth of character or situation; but it may also be an instrument for illusion. Though in one way a mirror presents us with the truth, cruelly or satisfyingly, it also shows shadow, not substance. We are aware of this fact in the carnival "funhouse"; too often, however, we are apt to equate a mere reflection, a play of light and shadow, with reality itself. Like Alice we believe that there must be a world correspondent to the one we call real, on the other side of the looking-glass.

What Bathsheba sees in her mirror is a handsome girl on a bright winter morning, but that this is her substantive nature, that her beauty and youth are her only reality, is an illusion. She later sees herself as the competent mistress of a large farm because those around her find it convenient to fall in with this notion, yet events show that she is no more mature as a landlord than as a farm-girl. She thinks she can indulge in such ill-advised pranks as sending Boldwood a Valentine, without serious consequences because she is deceived by his appearance of stability, not realizing that his nature is in a delicate state of equilibrium, like a bomb that is safe until one more atom is added beyond its critical mass. Despite everyone's contrary opinion and advice she thinks Troy a worthy man; and even after he has been proved otherwise she persists in believing in his love for her. Troy himself is illusioned—his attempt to right the wrong he has done Fanny by planting flowers on her grave is as patent a self-deception as Hardy can make it. The gargoyle which spouts its rainwater on the grave, washing the flowers away, is a clear enough indication of this. Boldwood is perhaps the most illusioned of all the characters in his infatuation for Bathsheba. Interestingly enough he also sees himself in a mirror, his square features transformed into something "wan in expression and insubstantial in form" (p. 114).

Note

1. All references to Thomas Hardy's works are to the Wessex Edition (London: Macmillan Publishing Co., 1912).

—Richard C. Carpenter, "The Mirror and the Sword: Imagery in *Far from the Madding Crowd*," *Nineteenth-Century Fiction* 18, no. 4 (March 1964): pp. 331–33, 335–36.

WILLIAM MISTICHELLI ON ANDROGYNY, SURVIVAL AND FULFILLMENT

[William Mistichelli is the author of "'This Pageantry of Fear': The Sublime in Thomas Hardy" (1996) and "The Trumpet Major's Signal: Kinship and Sexual Rivalry in the Novels of Thomas Hardy." In the excerpt below from his article, "Androgyny, Survival, and Fulfillment in Thomas Hardy's *Far From the Madding Crowd*," Mistichelli discusses the meaning of the recurring pattern of uncertainty and ambiguity in the sexual identities of the characters.]

In *Far From The Madding Crowd* uncertainty or ambiguity about sexual identities and roles becomes a recurring motif, especially in connection with the heroine, Bathsheba Everdene. Time and again in the novel, one encounters situations where outright confusion or some reversal of expectations about Bathsheba's sex produces significant revelations about her character and introduces important turns in her life. When she first comes to meet her workers as owner of the Weatherbury farm, she is referred to as *Sir* by Joseph Poorgrass (*Far From The Madding Crowd* 113; ch. 10). Another of her workers elsewhere separates her from the rest of her sex by noting with a mixture of surprise and respect that she doesn't tell women's lies (*Madding Crowd* 393; ch. 53). She is assumed to be a male thief or possibly a gypsy ("a woman was out of the question") when at night she takes a horse from her stables to meet Frank Troy at Bath (*Madding Crowd* 239; ch. 32). On her first encounter with Troy, as they bump in the dark, he asks if she is a woman, though she has already spoken (*Madding Crowd* 192; ch. 24).

Yet despite these misapprehensions about her sex and the inability of others to match her behavior with her sexual identity, she is extraordinarily attractive to men and deeply fond of "women's things." She is sought as a wife by three different suitors. She knits (*Madding Crowd* 187; ch. 23), loves flowers (346; ch. 46), and indulges in revealing female fancies and anxieties when she considers possible marriage to Boldwood (163; ch. 20) and Oak (66f.; ch. 4). The implications are strong everywhere in the novel that the responses Bathsheba provokes in others and the way she approaches life are in no way connected with a deficiency in her or an unattractive abnormality. Troy's reference to her as "mate" (192; ch. 24) makes this point in a subtle yet succinct way, though at the time he speaks it, he is ignorant of her identity. As a term commonly used for sailors and spouses, it draws together a wide range of possibilities about behavior, values, and attitudes that range from the love of daring and adventure to the need for stability and home life. Just as Bathsheba is called both "mate" and "Sir," so too is she alluded to as Amazonian (229, 30; ch. 30) and Eve-like (149; ch. 17). The pattern of references offers a profusion of meanings that discloses something in her that transcends rigidly conceptualized sexual boundaries. She is possessed, one might say, of a double sex, which is essential to her attractiveness to others and vital to her as a human agent.

Bathsheba's experience of her sexuality, though exceptional for its intensity and diversity, is not unique in the novel. The androgyny that is essential to her touches other characters, as well, in important ways. Fanny Robin courts Frank Troy's favors by throwing snow balls at his window (119f.; ch. 11). On their wedding day, Troy waits in vain at the church for Fanny to appear and leaves in anger because he believes he has been abandoned at the altar (ch. 16). Boldwood is mesmerized and made love-sick over a Valentine's day card from Bathsheba (ch. 14). Troy puts on her clothes to assist her in hiving (211; ch. 27). Oak is compared to a mother as he advises her about marriage (282; ch. 37). And it is Oak, the narrator makes it a point of saying, who blushes in Bathsheba's presence, not she in his (55; ch. 3).

The relevance of sexual mixing and reversal is at the center of the novel's action and theme. Androgyny in its various manifestations colors the conflicts which arise among the major characters and contributes significantly to their resolution. The transference of sexual traits—the adoption by women of attitudes or roles commonly held to be exclusively male, or vice-versa—in one sense promises a greater share of creative power and self-determination. At the same time, because these choices run counter to that which is socially condoned, they pose a serious threat to those who engage in them. Bathsheba's career, like that of all Hardy's major figures, is largely a matter of luck. Her story, and the story of others in the novel, are also, however, parables of survival and extinction. Androgyny informs the lives of these characters as a test of their adaptability and resilience. It indicates the degree to which they share in nature's power to renew itself against the forces of deterioration and death.

From the outset, Bathsheba is portrayed as an enigma who possesses an enormous capacity to attract. In a number of early scenes, she is described as Gabriel Oak observes her either from a distance or without her knowledge of his being there. Oak's responses on these occasions combine fascination and surprise. At the same time, they are shaped by traditional values and practical considerations. They become instrumental in this way as a means of introducing Bathsheba's behavior and character to the reader. When Oak first sees her, she is gazing in a mirror. He passes this off as simple vanity (44; ch. 1). From the narrator's following words, however, we gather that Oak's assessment is not to be taken as final:

> She [Bathsheba] simply observed herself as a fair product
> of Nature in the feminine kind, her thoughts seeming to
> glide into far-off though likely dramas in which men
> would play a part—vistas of probable triumphs—the
> smiles being of a phase suggesting that hearts were imag-
> ined as lost and won. (44)

Following this presentation of Bathsheba's reflections, we are offered
a disclaimer. What has been said of her, we are told, is "conjecture"
(44). Any claim to certainty concerning what lies at the heart of
Bathsheba's musing would be "rash" (44). The narrator's decision to
enlarge on Oak's reactions and then qualify his own account of
things dissipates the notion that any single assessment which presumes accuracy, such as Oak's, can be taken as satisfactory.

The issue is significant, since Oak sees Bathsheba as a creature
dominated by her sex, which means in his case, a stereotypical view
that she is almost certainly indulging her vanity, since she is a
woman. But Oak doesn't know her well enough at this time to make
responsible judgments about her character. The language of the narrator and his reluctance to support Oak offer us another Bathsheba
who is complex, hence more difficult to grasp than Oak presumes.
Her preoccupation in the passage with fantasy in the form of love
dramas carries with it a serious connection to real life. One recalls
that the plot of the novel renders her thoughts in some ways
prophetic. There is also present humor and irony, it seems, as she
smiles at "hearts . . . lost and won." Her appreciation of herself as a
"fair product" of the "feminine kind" appears somewhat detached
for a young woman presumably interested in reviewing her power to
attract the opposite sex. There may be vanity in it, but there is also
something more substantial which draws from real confidence in her
womanhood. The narrator speaks of how she "observed herself," as
though she were an object of scrutiny rather than infatuation. Concepts such as "fair product," "Nature," and "feminine kind" are both
general and abstract, therefore out of place in the daydreams of a
vain adolescent.

—William Mistichelli, "Androgyny, Survival, and Fulfillment in
Thomas Hardy's *Far From the Madding Crowd,*" *Modern Language
Studies* 18, no. 3 (Summer 1988): pp. 53–55.

[Michael Squires is the author of *The Pastoral Novel: Studies in George Eliot, Thomas Hardy and D. H. Lawrence* (1974) and the editor of *A Propos of Lady Chatterley's Lover/D. H. Lawrence* (1993). In the excerpt below from his article, "*Far from the Madding Crowd* as Modified Pastoral," Squires discusses Hardy's use of reworking of traditional pastoral setting and subjects as an "interpretive account of rural society."]

In a letter to Leslie Stephen, Hardy explained that his new novel was to be "a pastoral tale with the title of *Far from the Madding Crowd*" in which "the characters would probably be a young woman-farmer, a shepherd, and a sergeant of cavalry."[1] Hardy succeeded in his early intention of writing "a pastoral tale" in two respects. He wrote a novel about sheep and shepherds, the traditional pastoral subject; but he also wrote a novel at least partly in the traditional manner, by portraying rural life nostalgically and by stressing its beauty rather than its coarseness. The numerous pastoral scenes weave a solidly rural texture that has the smell of hay and the feel of fleece, and Hardy's knowledge of the agricultural world expresses itself in richly connotative prose that frequently crystallizes into poetry. Reminiscent and idealized, the result is a charming interpretive account of rural society.

Yet the falsification and artificiality of traditional pastoral have been rigorously excluded from Hardy's account. In *Far from the Madding Crowd* (1874) there is no perpetual summer, no frolicking sheep, no piping shepherds who live without care. Instead, there are many realistic details of actual rural life: sheep die, storms threaten, shepherds have misfortunes both "amorous and pastoral," peasants work, and unhappiness and despair are spattered over the second half of the story. Before the novel's essential realism, prettiness disappears. As William J. Hyde has shown, "a selective and discriminating use of the actual always forms the basis of [Hardy's] portraits."[2] Because these realistic details are not usually found in traditional pastoral literature, it is true that Hardy's novel is not traditional pastoral, but a modified version of traditional pastoral in which the manner and the underlying attitudes of pastoral are still present but in which real details of rural life form the substance of the work. Hardy's purpose, that is, was not to give a precise transcript of real rural life, but rather to select and to heighten those features which form a vital pattern of comprehension and meaning and which embody the value of what he saw as a pastoral world apart from urban society.[3] ⟨. . .⟩

Pastoral has in the twentieth century been subject to a wide range of critical definitions, depending on the aspects of pastoral that a critic stresses. The protean nature of the genre has in fact caused one writer to lament that "there are as many definitions as there are critics of pastoral."[4] W. W. Greg in his standard historical study *Pastoral Poetry and Pastoral Drama* (1906) defines pastoral in terms of its fundamental city–country contrast: "What does appear to be a constant element in the pastoral as known to literature is the recognition of contrast, implicit or expressed, between pastoral life and some more complex type of civilization."[5] Greg's basic definition of traditional pastoral was considerably modified by William Empson who, in *Some Versions of Pastoral* (1935), demonstrates that the pastoral of tradition survives in various mutations or "versions" beyond its brilliant Renaissance flowering. In diverse works Empson attempts to show "the ways in which the pastoral process of putting the complex into the simple" has been used in English literature.[6] Although he reduces the essence of pastoral to this loose and simple formula that can be applied to numerous works, he does succeed in broadening the traditional conception of pastoral. Frank Kermode, in his introduction to the anthology *English Pastoral Poetry* (1952), largely expands earlier ideas about pastoral. Defining pastoral as "literature which deals with rural life," Kermode, like Greg, focuses mainly on the city–country contrast as the essential element of pastoral by showing that pastoral flourishes at a moment in urban development when the tension between metropolis and country is still evident.[7] ⟨. . .⟩ *Far from the Madding Crowd*, though its tension between city and country is more complex than to sanction total condemnation, frequently registers such a criticism of urban life. ⟨. . .⟩

⟨. . .⟩ The term can signify city–country contrast, complexity viewed as simplicity, criticism of life, an economic idyll, universal experience seen through the medium of the rural world, perspective, or a pattern of escape, illumination, and return. Though the definitions of the term are diverse, we will take pastoral in this essay to mean the genre of literature which idealizes country life through the sharp contrast between city and country, the implied withdrawal from a complex to a simple world, the urban awareness of rural life and the resulting tension between value systems, the intense nostalgia for a Golden-Age past, and the creation of a circumscribed and remote pastoral world characterized by harmony between man and nature and by an atmosphere of idyllic contentment—a world in which country life, stripped of its coarsest features, is made palatable to urban society. With this definition in mind we will see that, by adding realism, by employing relatively few pastoral conventions, and by not insisting on an ironic view of life or on a return from the pastoral haven to the sophisticated world, *Far from the Madding Crowd* is not traditional pastoral, but a modified version of traditional pastoral.

Notes

1. Florence Emily Hardy, *The Life of Thomas Hardy* (New York, 1962), p. 95.

2. "Hardy's View of Realism: A Key to the Rustic Characters," *VS* 2 (September 1958): 56.

3. For a full discussion of the question of Hardy's realism, see Hyde's article (note 2 above): 45–59. He concludes in his study, however, that "a survey of the social and economic history of nineteenth-century English rural life will at times confirm Hardy's observations but will at the same time suggest the 'real' peasant beside whom Hardy's carefully chosen specimens must have appeared idealized to some of his contemporaries. Such a survey will encounter two major impressions that Hardy usually leaves out of focus: the animal nature of the peasant and the economic suffering of his lot" (48).

4. Robin Magowan, "Fromentin and Jewett: Pastoral Narrative in the Nineteenth Century," *Comparative Literature* 16 (Fall 1964): 331.

5. (Reprint ed., New York, 1959), p. 4.

6. (Reprint ed., Norfolk, Conn., New Directions Books, 1960), p. 23.

7. (London), p. 15.

—Michael Squires, "*Far from the Madding Crowd* as Modified Pastoral," *Nineteenth-Century Fiction* 25, no. 3 (December 1970): pp. 299–301, 303.

JUDITH BRYANT WITTENBERG ON ANGLES OF VISION

[Judith Bryant Wittenberg is an editor of *Unflinching Gaze: Morrison and Faulkner Re-Envisioned* (1997) and the author of *Faulkner: The Transfiguration of Biography* (1979). In the excerpt below from her article, "Angles of Vision and Questions of Gender in *Far from the Madding Crowd*," Wittenberg discusses Hardy's preoccupation with visual matters as a way of interpreting his attitude towards women.]

One of the more controversial issues in recent Hardy criticism concerns his attitudes toward and fictional treatments of women. For example, in a 1975 article, Katharine Rogers says that, although "Thomas Hardy repeatedly shaped his characters and plots to show his sympathy with women and his awareness of the disadvantages society laid upon them, . . . if we look beyond Hardy's conscious intentions to such things as repeated themes, incidental comments, and subtle differences in the presentation of analogous male and female characters, we find evidence that he could not altogether overcome the sexual stereotypes of his culture."[1] Despite the fact that critics are unlikely to reach any consensus on this topic in the near future, it remains a fruitful one. Readerly awareness of Hardy's ambivalence on this particular subject provides a useful avenue to understanding the sort of larger dialectic that gives his best fiction much of its tension and power. This essay will examine one aspect of Hardy's method—his preoccupation with sight-centered matters and their relationship to his depiction of women and their problems in *Far from the Madding Crowd*—and the way in which it embodies a dialogue having both philosophical and psychoanalytic implications that places Hardy's work in a larger context.

I.

Perception and its role in both intellectual and emotional development has been important to thinkers other than aesthetic theoreticians such as E. H. Gombrich and Rudolph Arnheim.[2] Several English philosophers, most notably John Locke, George Berkeley, and David Hume, all of whose works Hardy was familiar with, had, by the end of the eighteenth century, elaborated upon the compelling problems of epistemological definition in a Cartesian universe and collectively posited a world in which the seeing "eye" was the point of origin for the knowing "I." Later psychoanalytic theorists, some of whose work Hardy anticipates in intriguing ways,[3] such as Freud, regarded the drive to see as fundamental to the instinct for knowledge and as basic to the process of awakening desire for the love-object during later sexual development.[4] Thus the eye becomes throughout life, particularly for males, one of the important erotogenic zones.[5] Seeing can also, of course, lead to trauma and thence to neurosis or perversion.[6]

While much of Hardy's fiction is informed by post-Lockean and psychoanalytic theories of seeing, *Far from the Madding Crowd* (1874), his fourth published novel and the first great work of his career, represents a culmination of his treatment of the various visual preoccupations that are evident in all the work of his early period. Persistently and complexly present in the text are several thematic and technical elements arising from Hardy's concepts of the individual eye as the inlet of sense knowledge and as a sexual force, of the way in which one's sense of self is essentially created in perceptual moments, and of the collective eye as the locus of moral judgment; moreover, Hardy relates such issues in intriguing ways to questions of gender and control. Though these elements are clearly subordinated to the story, they underlie both its basic assumptions and its presentation.

The early pages of the novel serve in this respect as a paradigm both of the entire work and of all Hardy's fiction of this period, compressing an extraordinary number of sight-centered components into our introduction to Gabriel Oak and Oak's meeting with Bathsheba Everdene and linking them to crucial aspects of male and female roles. They constitute a rich exemplification of Hardy's conception of the complex role which vision plays in life and in the fiction-making process. Several physical points of station (i.e., the distance of the spectator from the nearest point of the "picture" he sees), each with significant implications, are juxtaposed in these opening pages, the first of them, that of the narrator, being the most important to this and all of Hardy's fiction. The spectatorial narrator begins by offering a Halsian portrait of a ruddy, smiling Oak that obviously applies to the general as well as the specific instance, going on, in a confident, somewhat amused tone, to describe Oak's behavior, character, and religious views, contrasting the limited "mental picture formed by his neighbours" with the things available to the notice of "thoughtful persons" (p. 2), among whom the narrator obviously belongs.[7]

Oak's point of view is the second one offered and the second in importance. Hardy shifts us to him, "glancing over the hedge" in a typical voyeuristic moment of the benign variety. He sees Bathsheba preening on her wagon and judges her as vain, remaining himself seemingly unaroused, but the more libidinal moments of peeping which immediately follow are portended by the cat who "affectionately survey[s] the small birds around." Women are often identified with birds in Hardy's fiction (as in much earlier writing in English), and the cat's gaze, though idle, is unquestionably predatory, like the male gaze.

Notes

1. Katharine Rogers, "Women in Thomas Hardy," *Centennial Review*, 19 (1975), 249–58.

2. In E. H. Gombrich, *Art and Illusion* (New York: Bollingen, 1965), and Rudolph Arnheim, *Art and Visual Perception* (Berkeley: University of California Press, 1954).

3. See Rosemary Sumner, *Thomas Hardy: Psychological Novelist* (New York: St. Martin's, 1981).

4. *The Standard Edition of the Complete Works of Sigmund Freud*, trans. James Strachey (London: Hogarth, 1953), VII, p. 156.

5. See, for example, Sandor Ferenczi, "On Eye Symbolism," in *First Contributions to Psychoanalysis*, trans. Ernest Jones (London: Hogarth, 1952), pp. 270–276.

6. See Otto Fenichel, *The Psychoanalytic Theory of Neurosis* (New York: Norton, 1945), pp. 71–2, 92, 345–9; Otto Fenichel, "The Scoptophilic Instinct and Identification," *Collected Papers*, First Series (New York: Norton, 1953); David W. Allen, *The Fear of Looking* (Charlottesville: University of Virginia Press, 1974).

7. All page references are to the Wessex Edition (London: Macmillan, 1912–31). The spectatorial quality of Hardy's narrator has been commented on by, for example, J. Hillis Miller, *Thomas Hardy: Distance and Desire* (Cambridge: Belknap Press of Harvard University Press, 1970), pp. xii, 7; and David Lodge, "Thomas Hardy and Cinematographic Form," *Novel*, 7 (1974), 250.

—Judith Bryant Wittenberg, "Angles of Vision and Questions of Gender in *Far from the Madding Crowd*," *The Centennial Review* 30, no. 1 (Winter 1986): pp. 25–27.

Plot Summary of
The Return of the Native

Published in 1878, Hardy began writing *The Return of the Native* in the summer of 1877, upon his return from a tour of Holland and the Rhine valley with his wife. Serialized in *Belgravia* during January–December 1878, the novel is testimony to a resurgence in imaginative force and is set in a landscape steeped in early memories. Set amongst the heathcroppers, reddlemen and mummers, whom his grandmother remembered, *The Return of the Native* includes stories of witchcraft and superstitious practices. Clym's foregoing of his career in the city is reminiscent of Hardy's own abandonment of architecture. *The Return of the Native* is a melodramatic novel, set in the 1840s and overshadowed by the lowering presence of Egdon Heath. In a happy ending (forced on Hardy by his magazine editor), Diggory Venn marries the widowed Thomasin. In his 1895 preface, Hardy draws the analogy between his novel and Shakespeare's *King Lear*, "that traditionary King of Wessex," also associated with heaths.

Book First: The Three Women. As Book First opens onto Egdon Heath, we enter a dark and brooding landscape, a "vast tract of unenclosed wild," a landscape which is to play a predominant role in the fate of its inhabitants, so much so that the Heath is given human attributes with a personality to be reckoned with. "The face of the heath by its mere complexion added half an hour to evening; it could in like manner retard the dawn, sadden noon, [and] anticipate the frowning of storms scarcely generated. . . ." It is twilight on a Saturday in November in a land which remains hostile towards the encroachment of civilization, tenaciously clinging to "the same antique brown dress, the natural and invariable garment," providing "a certain vein of satire on human vanity in clothes." It is here that we are introduced to a young man of twenty-four, Diggory Venn, who, like the landscape he traverses, hearkens back to a much earlier time and simpler existence. He is a reddleman, one who sells the red chalk used to mark sheep, an occupation which is "a curious, interesting, and nearly perished link between obsolete forms of life and those which generally prevail." Mr. Venn is crossing the heath in "a lurid red" covered wagon (the wagon having derived its color from his trade), with a young woman (Thomasin Yeobright) whose identity he conceals from an old man he encounters on the heath. As he continues his travels, Mr. Venn notices the figure of a woman atop a Celtic barrow, a high hill which in prehistoric times was the site of a burial mound. She is then displaced by a group of "burdened figures,"—heath folk who have come to start a Fifth of November bonfire. Included in this group are Timothy Fairway, Grandfer Cantle, Christian Cantle, Humphrey, Olly Dowden and Susan Nonsuch. And as they watch the fire, they discuss the upcoming marriage of Thomasin Yeobright and Damon Wildeve, a man who moved "with the pantomimic expression of a lady-killing career,"—an engineer turned innkeeper at the Quiet Woman Inn. As it turns out, Wildeve has not married her as promised, claiming that the marriage license was wrong and could not be rectified on their anticipated wedding day. Wildeve is then revealed to have had a rendezvous with his former lover, Eustacia Vye, and wishes for her to run off with him to America. At the same time, we learn that Diggory Venn is a former, albeit unsuccessful, suitor of Thomasin Yeobright. Having overheard a conversation between Wildeve and Eustacia, Venn decides to pursue Thomasin's hand in marriage once again, but is rebuffed.

Book Second: The Arrival. The second book begins with Clym Yeobright's anticipated return from Paris to Egdon Heath for the Christmas holiday. While Mrs. Yeobright and her niece, Thomasin, are preparing the house, getting apples from the loft and holly and berries from the heath, Eustacia launches into reverie about Clym returning from the fantastic world of Paris—a vision which reminds her of the preface to James Thomson's allegorical poem, The Castle of Indolence (1748) "at which myriads of imprisoned shapes arose where had previously appeared the stillness of a void." When Eustacia does walk down towards the Yeobright house to catch a first glimpse of Clym on the heath, she is only able to hear his voice. "All emotional things were possible to the speaker of that 'good night.' Eustacia's imagination supplied the rest. . . ." However, Eustacia soon finds a way to encounter Clym by taking Charley's place at a Christmas mummer's play, more specifically, "the well-known play of 'St. George.'" The original meaning of "mummer" is of Danish origin, denoting one who wears a mask, and Eustacia's plan is to be disguised in Charley's costume as the Turkish Knight, St. George's adversary, dressed in masculine attire with "strips of ribbon [which] were used to cover the face in mumming costumes, representing the barred visor of the mediaeval helment." But her male disguise soon becomes an obstacle rather than an advantage, as Eustacia can only observe and grow anxious that Clym and his cousin Thomasin may fall in love. "What a sheer waste of herself to be dressed thus while another was shining to advantage!" When Eustacia rushes out, Clym quickly suspects that she is a woman and engages her in conversation. As it turns out, Eustacia begins to question the reality of Clym as opposed to the fantasy she has thus far been entertaining. She begins to realize that Clym is really a total stranger to her. After she parts from Clym and winds her way home, Eustacia remembers, and just as quickly dismisses, the fact that she was supposed to meet Wildeve on the heath. "Wildeve had at present the rayless outline of the sun through smoked glass." Eustacia is now prepared, with Venn's further assistance, to try to promote a romance between Wildeve and Thomasin, fearing that the young Miss Yeobright could well become her romantic rival for Clym's affections. With this scheme in mind, Eustacia writes a letter to Wildeve, delivered by the willing and impartial assistance of Diggory Venn. As Eustacia ponders his character and remarks "[w]hat a strange sort of love, to be entirely free from that quality of selfishness which is frequently the chief constituent of the passion, and sometimes its only one," these thoughts have the quality of an auspicious omen for the young man's ultimate happiness. For his part, Wildeve is determined to seek revenge on Eustacia. Indeed, he appears to be the exact opposite of Venn when we are told that "[f]ull of this resolve to marry [Thomasin] in haste, and wring the heart of the proud girl [Eustacia], Wildeve went on his way." And, as a further inducement to this romantic arrangement, Clym, while away from home, adds his encouragement to such a union. For her part, Thomasin wants a simple and fast marriage, to take place before Clym's return home, which it does.

Book Third: The Fascination. The third book opens with a description of the worldly Clym's physical appearance and, through a series of artistic and historical analogies, Hardy uses his vast knowledge and learning about art and history to render the encroachment of modern civilization. "In Clym Yeobright's face could be dimly seen the typical countenance of the future." And in so doing, Hardy is providing a commentary on the character of Egdon Heath and the rustic simplicity which is being threatened by the notion of progress. "The truth seems to be that a long line of dillusive centuries has permanently displaced the Hellenic idea of life. . . . That old-fashioned revelling in the general situation grows less and less possible as we uncover the defects of natural laws, and see the quandary that man is in by their operation." Indeed, the community of heath dwellers consider Clym a rather special person not only because as a boy great things were expected, "that he would be successful in an unusual way," but also because of his position in the diamond business in far-off Paris, a trade "whose sole concern was with the especial symbols of self-indulgence and vainglory." While at a haircutting at Fairways, Clym attempts to explain to the group that he has come home to make himself into a schoolteacher—they do not believe him. "'A man who is doing well elsewhere wouldn't bide here two or three weeks for nothing,' said Fairway." Neither does Mrs. Yeobright believe him, but, in her case, suspicions are self-imposed rather than based on any actual reason. The conversation between them in which he tries to persuade them about his change in career is interrupted by Christian Cantle who now relates the tale of Eustacia's being pricked in the arm with a stocking needle by Susan Nunsuch, a revenge the latter has planned because she is convinced Eustacia has bewitched her children. Clym, who has yet to meet Eustacia, now begins to question whether she was the woman whom he met disguised as a mummer. When he does encounter her, he tries to get her to admit that she was one of the mummers whom he had met. His meetings with Eustacia also continue despite Mrs. Yeobright's protests, and an increasing tension begins to form between mother and son, at Clym's "ill-timed betrayal of feeling for a new woman." Eustacia is determined to pursue her own agenda to marry Clym and persuade him to return to Paris—to the "world of historical romance." Most importantly, however, this is a narrative of endlessly shifting romantic liaisons in which fate is the preeminent governing force determining the destiny of these erstwhile lovers. And to this end of demonstrating the tyranny of fate, Hardy weaves a multitude of narrative detours; which, among other things, are prophetic for the protagonists. In this third book, one of those detours occurs as Mrs. Yeobright entrusts Christian Cantle, rather than Wildeve, to deliver money to Thomasin and Clym. Christian (accompanied by Wildeve) first meets up with a group going to a raffle at The Quiet Woman Inn and wins a pair of dice, only to be seduced by his luck, and eager to gamble with Wildeve, the latter managing to win all the money. However, Venn, who has been observing this transaction from the shadows, turns up to challenge Wildeve and manages to win the entire 100 guineas back, delivering the entire sum to Thomasin. "Thus Venn, in his anxiety to rectify matters, had placed in Thomasin's hands not only the fifty guineas which rightly belonged to her, but also the fifty intended for her cousin Clym."

Book Fourth: The Closed Door begins with Clym and Eustacia living a secluded life in the house at Alderworth, "with a monotony which was delightful to them." Clym continues his studies while Eustacia maintains her hopes that they will get to Paris. "She had calculated to such a degree on the probability of success that she had represented Paris, and not Budmouth, to her grandfather as in all likelihood their future home." In the meantime, Mrs. Yeobright is baffled that Clym has never acknowledged receipt of the guineas until Christian tells her that Wildeve won the money in a gambling transaction. She decides to call on Eustacia who at this time is completely unaware of the money as none of it ever reached Clym. Thus, Eustacia misconstrues the older woman's questions, and the two women quarrel bitterly. "'I am only a poor old woman who has lost a son.'" In another prophetic detail, Clym develops an acute eye inflammation brought about by too many hours spent reading, "a morbid sensibility to light," and takes up furze cutting with Humphrey, while Eustacia becomes very depressed. "That dream of Paris was not likely to cohere into substance in the presence of this misfortune." And, as an antidote to her depression, Eustacia takes up "gipysing" dancing, "[a] whole village-full of sensuous emotion" in East Egdon where she is surprised to find Wildeve. "Wildeve by himself would have been merely an agitation; Wildeve added to the dance and the moonlight, and the secrecy, began to be a delight." However, Venn, who is forever witnessing disturbing events and "illicit" liaisons, is sure that he has seen Eustacia walking with Wildeve, and sets out to confirm as much. And Mrs. Yeobright, determined to be reconciled with her son, sets out for Clym's residence in Alderworth where she observes, through a clump of trees, Wildeve calling on Eustacia. Not realizing that Clym is asleep, Mrs. Yeobright becomes very upset that Eustacia will not answer her knock on the door, blaming her son for allowing this to happen. "'Tis too much—Clym, how can he bear to do it! He is at home; and yet he lets her shut the door against me!'" When Clym learns of her attempted visit, he sets out to see his mother, where he finds her lying prostrate near Blooms-End. While he seeks help, Mrs. Yeobright is bitten by an adder, which he treats with the fat of another adder, "the old remedy of the viper-catchers," but Mrs. Yeobright soon dies. While Eustacia and Wildeve (who has now inherited eleven thousand pounds) watch undetected from a vantage point behind the hut, Susan Nunsuch's boy delivers a final message from Mrs. Yeobright. "'That woman asleep there walked along with me today; and she said I was to say that I had seed her, and she was a broken-hearted woman and cast off by her son.'"

Book Fifth: The Discovery. The fifth book begins with Clym becoming ill and irrational, for several weeks following his mother's death. He is, indeed, beyond consolation, blaming himself for her death. "'What's the moon to a man like me? Let it shine—let anything be, so that I never see another day!'" In the meantime, Wildeve counsels Eustacia never to admit to Clym that her former lover was in the house at the time Mrs. Yeobright was knocking at the door. When Clym finally recovers, he questions Christian, who has come to announce the birth of Thomasin's child, from whom he learns that his mother had planned to visit him and further discovers from Venn that she was ready to forgive her estranged son. It is then only a short time before Clym accuses Eustacia of cruelty to his mother, and deceiving him with another man. Clym flies into a terrible rage, although he refrains from striking her while Eustacia returns to her grandfather's house where she is cared for by Charley, a former admirer. In an unsuccessful attempt to cheer her up, Charley builds a bonfire for her, not realizing that she hopes Wildeve will read it as a plea for his return. The signal works and Wildeve returns, wanting to assist her in any way possible. On the next evening, a letter arrives from Clym, and when Captain Vye finally decides to deliver it to Eustacia, she has already left the house. It is raining on the heath and Eustacia is feeling utterly hopeless. "Never was harmony more perfect than that between the chaos of her mind and the chaos of the world without." At the same time, having spotted Eustacia, Susan Nunsuch devises a wax effigy of her, sticking it with pins and burning it in a fire, all the while murmuring to herself. "It was a strange jargon—the Lord's Prayer repeated backwards—the incantation usual in proceedings for obtaining unhallowed assistance against any enemy." In the meantime, Thomasin and Captain Vye tell Clym of Eustacia's inclination to commit suicide using her grandfather's pistols. After the two men leave, Thomasin eventually sets out for The Quiet Woman with her child and on the way meets Venn who accompanies her to the inn where Wildeve is awaiting

Eustacia. As Clym approaches Wildeve, they hear the sound of a body falling into the stream adjoining Shadwater Weir. "Across this gashed and puckered mirror a dark body was slowly borne by one of the backward currents." Both men jump in hoping to save her. With Venn's able assistance, Clym is rescued and Eustacia's body is retrieved. Wildeve, however, does not survive.

Book Sixth: Aftercourses. Following Wildeve's death, Thomasin receives a small inheritance, and decides to move in with Clym. For his part, Clym is now occupying his time in preparing for his vocation as preacher. Diggory Venn, who is now a dairy farmer, calls upon Thomasin and she is pleased to see him. The village is preparing for Maypole Day. "The instincts of merry England lingered on here with exceptional vitality, and the symbolic customs which tradition has attached to each season of the year were yet a reality on Egdon." During the festivities, Venn manages to obtain one of Thomasin's gloves, worn by her servant girl, though Thomasin herself does not attend. After discovering from the servant what Venn has done, Thomasin encounters him while taking her daughter Eustacia for an airing. They see each other after this meeting. In the meantime, thinking he is obligated to do so because of his mother's wishes when she was alive, Clym is about to ask Thomasin to marry him, thinking he is obligated to fulfill his mother's wishes. But Thomasin tells him she wants to marry Venn. Although at first he disapproves, Clym offers no obstacle to Thomasin's marrying Venn. Clym, has lost all passion with the death of Eustacia. "Every pulse of loverlike feeling which had not been stilled during Eustacia's lifetime had gone into the grave with her." He is last seen on top of Rainbarrow, performing as an itinerant preacher of moral lectures. "He left alone creeds and systems of philosophy, finding enough and more than enough to occupy his tongue in the opinions and actions common to all good men." ❁

List of Characters in
The Return of the Native

Eustacia Vye – A young woman of nineteen who longs to leave the dismal life of the heath for the excitement of city life. Both an independent and unconventional spirit, she is overly passionate and obsessed with her own needs. Though she is often the victim of her own illusions, she is nevertheless realistic and honest with herself. Just before her death she cries out, "How I have tried and tried to be a splendid woman, and how destiny has been against me! . . . I do not deserve my lot!"

Damon Wildeve – A romantic man, Wildeve appears to be far too sophisticated for the simple rural folk of Egdon. A man with a shady past, he has failed at his career as an engineer, but seems always to succeed with women. He seems to have neither friends nor family connections. Hardy depicts him as acting impulsively and selfishly. Though he is not evil, his narcissism hurts others.

Thomasin Yeobright – A countrified and inexperienced young woman, Thomasin appears to be less passionate than Eustacia, less profound than Clym, and less sophisticated than Wildeve. Neither does she possess Mrs. Yeobright's insightfulness. Neverthless, Thomasin is the one who achieves a conventionally happy life. She is rooted to the heath and happy to live a simple life.

Clym Yeobright – A well-meaning and intelligent young man, Clym Yeobright dislikes the city life he left behind in Paris, yet no one in Egdon understands his aspiration to teach school. Neither does Clym really know himself. His ideas come from books rather than from experience. Though he thinks of himself as rational, his love for Eustacia causes him to act rashly. The most important influence in his life is his home, especially his mother, Mrs. Yeobright.

Mrs. Yeobright – As Clym's mother she is snobbish, even though her social position outside Egdon is unremarkable. A very stubborn woman who likes getting her own way, she meddles in other peoples lives, especially Clym's, with disastrous results. Neverthless, she has amazingly accurate judgment, and her love for Clym and Thomasin always wins out. She is very much at home in the Egdon community.

Diggory Venn – Resourceful and sophisticated he is a very competent man of twenty-four who earns his living as a reddleman. Strong, silent and loyal, Diggory Venn is an angelic being, with the highest of ethical standards. He seems to always arrive just at the right moment to rescue Thomasin.

Captain Vye – Eustacia's grandfather, a retired sailor.

Timothy Fairway – A furze dealer and a pompous, sententious man of middle age who is greatly respected by the other heath folk.

Grandfer Cantle – A somewhat senile and lively old soldier about sixty-nine years in age.

Christian Cantle – Grandfer Cantle's fearful and timid thirty-one year-old son.

Humphrey – A furze cutter.

Sam – A turf cutter.

Susan Nunsuch – A superstitious woman who suspects Eustacia of being a witch and of casting evil spells on her son.

Olly Dowden – A besom (heath broom) maker.

Charley – A sixteen year-old boy working for Captain Vye, he admires Eustacia, largely from afar. ❀

Critical Views on
The Return of the Native

GILLIAN BEER ON PLOT AND WRITING

[Gillian Beer is the author of *Open Fields: Science in Cultural Encounter* (1996) and *Forging the Missing Link: Interdisciplinary Stories* (1992). In the excerpt below from the chapter entitled "Finding a Scale for the Human: Plot and Writing in Hardy's Novels," Beer discusses the nature of human happiness and the influence of Darwin's theories in Hardy's work.]

The emphasis upon systems more extensive than the life span of the individual and little according to his needs is essential to Hardy's insight. Much of the grandeur of his fiction comes from his acceptance of people's independence and self-assertion—doomed and curtailed persistently, but recuperating. But further underlying that emphasis upon the individual is the paradox that even those recuperative energies are there primarily to serve the longer needs of the race and are part of a procreative energy designed to combat extinction, not the death of any individual.

Alongside the emphasis on apprehension and anxiety, on inevitable overthrow long foreseen, persistingly evaded, there is, however, another prevailing sensation in Hardy's work equally strongly related to his understanding of Darwin. It is that of happiness. Alongside the doomed sense of weighted past and incipient conclusion, goes a sense of plenitude, an 'appetite for joy'. This finds expression—as it must if at all—in the moment-by-moment fullness of the text. In 'Song of Myself' Whitman (who is quoted in *Tess*) wrote:

> I have heard what the talkers were talking, the talk of the
>   beginning
>   and the end,
> But I do not talk of the beginning or the end.
> There was never any more inception than there is now,
> Nor any more youth and age than there is now,
> And will never be any more perfection than there is now,
> Nor any more heaven or hell than there is now.

Urge and urge and urge,
Always the procreant urge of the world.

At each moment the world is complete, though urged onwards always by procreation. Whitman's is a powerful alternative to that form of evolutionary thinking which sets the past aspiring to become present, and the present imagining a more satisfying future. Whitman's sense of the world's fullness is yet linked to that 'appetite for joy' which Hardy saw as charging life equally with rapture and disaster. Sexual joy is always dangerous, not only because of the possibility of loss, but because it is linked to *generation,* the law which rides like a juggernaut over and through individual identity and individual life spans. ⟨. . .⟩

The impassioned moment is seized through touch and temperature, the most intimately present of sense-experience. Then the language turns aside, first into the imagery of the sea and of motion (still perpetuating the bodily experience of the lovers). The sense of power and of helplessness change into the jarring abstraction of the 'vague lucubrations over the social rubric', facetiously orotund. The reader must work for meaning, instead of being immersed in meaning—and the sense and sound alike rebuff readers, and distance lovers.

Hardy comments on another natural drive, separate from that of procreation although often associated with it: 'the determination to enjoy': 'Thought of the determination to enjoy. We see it in all nature, from the leaf on the tree to the titled lady at the ball . . . Like pent-up water it will find a chink of possibility somewhere' (August 1888). In 'The Dorsetshire Labourer' (1883) he sees the refusal to believe in happiness among 'the labouring classes' as a class-bound condescension and satirises such views:

> Misery and fever lurk in his cottage, while to paraphrase
> the words of a recent writer on the labouring classes, in his
> future there are only the workshop and the grave. He
> hardly dares to think at all. He has few thoughts of joy, and
> little hope of rest. ⟨. . .⟩

⟨Hardy⟩ describes not only the 'fearful joy', the 'killing joy' of sexual arousal, but placable, unnoticed happiness, something so 'matter of course' that no one comments on it. So only Eustacia sets out to *act* in the Mummers' play; the rest go through the motions in a way which Hardy thoroughly naturalises by means of the metaphor of mushrooms:

> The remainder of the play ended: the Saracen's head was cut off, and Saint George stood as victor. Nobody commented, any more than they would have commented on the fact of mushrooms coming in autumn or snowdrops in spring. They took the piece as phlegmatically as did the actors themselves. It was a phase of cheerfulness which was, as a matter of course, to be passed through every Christmas; and there was no more to be said. (*Return:* 157) ⟨...⟩

Hardy like Darwin places himself in his texts as observer, traveller, a conditional presence capable of seeing things from multiple distances and diverse perspectives almost in the same moment.

> A traveller who should walk and observe any of these visitants as Venn observed them now could feel himself to be in direct communication with regions unknown to man. Here in front of him was a wild mallard—just arrived from the home of the north wind. The creature brought within him an amplitude of Northern knowledge. Glacial catastrophes, snow-storm episodes, glittering auroral effects, Polaris in the zenith, Franklin underfoot,—the category of his commonplaces was wonderful. But the bird, like many other philosophers, seemed as he looked at the reddleman to think that a present moment of comfortable reality was worth a decade of memories. (*Return:* 109)

The eye of the writing moves far and near, not so much dwelling in multiple minds, as in George Eliot, as creating a shifting space and changing scales. Ear and touch become identified.

> Throughout the blowing of these plaintive November winds that note bore a great resemblance to the ruins of human song which remain to the throat of fourscore and ten. It was a worn whisper, dry and papery, and it brushed so distinctly across the ear that, by the accustomed, the material minutiae in which it originated could be realized as by touch. It was the united products of infinitesimal vegetable causes, and these were neither stems, leaves, fruit, blades, prickles, lichen, nor moss.
> They were the mummied heath-bells of the past summer, originally tender and purple, now washed colour-

less by Michaelmas rains, and dried to dead skins by October suns. So low was an individual sound from these that a combination of hundreds only just emerged from silence, and the myriads of the whole declivity reached the woman's ear but as a shrivelled and intermittent recitative. Yet scarcely a single accent among the many afloat to-night could have such power to impress a listener with thoughts of its origin. One inwardly saw the infinity of those combined multitudes; and perceived that each of the tiny trumpets was seized on, entered, scoured and emerged from by the wind as thoroughly as if it were as vast as a crater. (*Return:* 78)

This vacillation of memory and material, near and far, of tactile and abstract makes for a kind of liberty for the reader, even though an unstable liberty. It is something to set against the dogged interpenetration of event by which his plots overdetermine outcome. We always sustain until the last moment a passionate sense of possible happiness: he sustains hope by different levels of plot, liberty by multiple perspectives. And the drive of his plots is so crushing precisely because of the full sense of *life* elated in us by the range of sense perceptions which are evoked through his writing. The intricate affinity of touch and sound keeps the reader alert and close. Looking back on a novel by Hardy many readers are afflicted and aghast. But he is also one of the most popular and widely read of writers: we enter his works not only to be chagrined and thwarted, but also sustained by the moment-by-moment plenitude of experience offered us. Traumatised by conclusion, the reader in retrospect almost forgets the bounty of text. Forgetting and having are both crucial in Hardy. ⟨...⟩

Two elements of Darwin's theory had a peculiarly personal significance in Hardy's writing—and they were elements which pointed in differing directions, forming a contradiction where Hardy could work. The first element was Darwin's insistence on 'normative felicity': despite the suffering in the natural world, survival depended on a deep association of life and pleasurability. ⟨...⟩

Instead of man disjunct from all other aspects of the material order, or at the pinnacle of hierarchy, he must now find a place in a world of 'horizontality', as it comes home to Clym in *The Return of the Native.* 'It gave him a sense of bare equality with, and no superiority to, a single living thing under the sun.'

So the problem of finding a scale for the human becomes a beset-
ting preoccupation of Hardy's work, a scale that will be neither
unrealistically grandiose, nor debilitatingly reductive, which will
accept evanescence and the autonomy of systems not serving the
human, but which will still call upon Darwin's often-repeated assertion: 'the relation of organism to organism is the most important of
all relations' (e.g. 14:449). Darwin offers no privileged place to the
human, but by appropriating older myth-metaphors such as the tree
of life, he might seem to restore a continuity or wholeness to the
human. In *The Woodlanders* Hardy reuses the image of the tree, first
in the abbreviated anthropological/psychological riposte of the old
man whose life is literally dependent on the tree which has grown
alongside his life's span; then through the entire imagery of work
which places the human at the service of the natural world, and
most strikingly in passages such as this, in which the human is seen
as part of (not fully in control of) natural process. The human body
is everywhere suggested in the description, the perfect exists alongside the warped and stunted; sound and touch are scarcely separable:

> They went noiselessly over mats of starry moss, rus-
> tled through interspersed tracts of leaves, skirted
> trunks with spreading roots whose mossed rinds
> made them like hands wearing green gloves; elbowed
> old elms and ashes with great forks, in which stood
> pools of water that overflowed on rainy days and ran
> down their stems in green cascades. On older trees
> still than these huge lobes of fungi grew like lungs.
> Here, as everywhere, the Unfulfilled Intention, which
> makes life what it is, was as obvious as it could be
> among the depraved crowds of a city slum. The leaf
> was deformed, the curve was crippled, the taper was
> interrupted; the lichen ate the vigour of the stalk, and
> the ivy strangled to death the promising sapling. (82)

—Gillian Beer, *Darwin's Plots: Evolutionary Narrative in Darwin,
George Eliot and Nineteenth-Century Fiction* (Cambridge: Cambridge
University Press, 2000): pp. 224–26; 230–33.

JENNIFER GRIBBLE ON THE AMBIGUITY OF "THE QUIET WOMAN"

[Jennifer Gribble is the editor of George Eliot's *Scenes of Clerical Life* (1998) and the author of *The Lady of Shallot in the Victorian Novel* (1983). In the excerpt below from her article, "The Quiet Women of Egdon Heath," Gribble discusses Hardy's 1912 edition in terms of the ambiguity of the inn sign at "The Quiet Woman" which beckons the traveler to a place of domestic respite while, simultaneously, undermining that promise by the image of the woman's severed head.]

Revising *The Return of the Native* for the 1912 Macmillan Wessex edition, Hardy adds this couplet to Damon Wildeve's inn sign at 'The Quiet Woman':

SINCE THE WOMAN'S QUIET

LET NO MAN BREED A RIOT

The earlier description of the sign as 'the figure of a matron carrying her head under her arm' is further reinforced by the adjective 'gruesome'. A footnote in the 1912 revision goes on to explain that 'the inn which really bore this sign and legend stood some miles to the north-west of the present scene'. It may be, as Simon Gatrell suggests, that these alterations were mostly directed towards ensuring that literary pilgrims in search of Egdon Heath could track it through 'observable geographic spaces'. It seems likely, however, that re-reading his novel more than thirty years after its first appearance in the 1878 numbers of *Belgravia,* Hardy perceived how the sardonic rhyme would underline the novel's thinking about the silence and the silencing of its quiet and unquiet women. On the face of it, the apparently neat fit between the sign's folk wisdom and the plot of the novel might seem to justify those readers who see Hardy as constrained by his culture's stereotypes of women, or by negative 'neutralizing structures' forced on him by his particular ideological moment. Clym Yeobright, believing that he has 'driven two women to their deaths' (p. 469) himself survives peaceably enough, indeed, to discourse in fable form on his mother's terminal silencing: 'ask on, my mother: for I will not say thee nay' (p. 482).

It turns out to be a sign that points in more than one direction: first inward, towards the inn, that traditional refuge from the female and the domestic, which nevertheless offers its comforts with the sign of the woman. Convivial talk on Egdon, we note, will drift as like as not into the pleasures and pains of conjugal life, a subject for anecdote and wonder. The sign points backwards too, to the oral culture within which Hardy's narrative will place itself, as well as outwards to continuing questions about gender stereotyping; the image of the silenced woman conflates both scold and temptress. Uncoupled from the traditional headship of the male, her disruptive potentiality put to rest, she obligingly carries her own severed head. To the pictured narrative, the couplet adds its own riddling wit. 'Breed' indicates at one and the same time procreative needs and the subversiveness of sexual interdependence. The riotousness of man seems to take its cue from the unruliness of woman, but whether as cause or consequence, who can say?

The equivocations of Hardy's sign graphically represent his interest in the teasing qualities of narrative—of how much will always fall away into silence or hint at what remains inexpressible or defy political readings, of what its apparent repetitions across time might have to say to its contemporary readership. In exploring sexual disgrace and the female unruliness which are the two sides of the quiet woman sign, Hardy returns with a narrative purpose often denied this novel, to 'the customs of the country', its rituals and ballads and village anecdotes. 'Trouble' is dramatized as energy—sexual energy most notably, as part of that beat of time through song and season that celebrates continuity and renewal on Egdon Heath.

It must be said that Clym's wife and mother are among Hardy's least quiet women. Mrs. Yeobright, 'a matron with a tang in her tongue', takes her outspokenness into the very church, rising to forbid the banns between Wildeve and her niece Tamsin. Eustacia Vye's challenges to contemporary decorum include speaking as a man while 'figuring in breeches' (p. 174). But the reader's imagination is equally held by their silencing: 'a woman's face looking at me through the window frame' (p. 337) sends Mrs. Yeobright to her death; Clym's last glimpse of Eustacia leaving their home dissolves into her death mask, 'caught in a momentary transition between fervour and resignation' (p. 446). Some of the novel's most crucial developments depend on withheld speech; the 'oral tradition' on which it draws disseminates inarticulate meanings; ancient rituals communicate tacitly, and the heath itself emerges from silence into 'wild rhetoric', endowed with the voices of pain and of jubilee. ⟨. . .⟩

Hardy needs no new historicist to instruct him that the time, place, physical laws and conditions and social customs and beliefs of the teller will help to shape the story told since that is the burden of this opening. It is far from being just 'a long descriptive essay on an empty landscape'. The whole novel, indeed, is charged with the recognition that we have no moment other than our own through which to grasp that story. This perception is struggled with, and flowers, most poignantly, in the Poems of 1912–13: if landscape is the indifferent record of aeons of story, it must also bear witness to the transitory story 'that we two passed'. The return of the literary consciousness to its native heath is clearly Hardy's drama as well as Clym Yeobright's. The vatic mood of this opening suggests that its strains are in part those of Hardy's historical moment, as the wisdom of Wordsworth's Nature confronts the impassive indifference of Darwin's.

—Jennifer Gribble, "The Quiet Women of Egdon Heath," *Essays in Criticism* 46, no. 3 (July 1996): pp. 234–37.

ROBERT LANGBAUM ON VERSIONS OF PASTORAL

[Robert Langbaum is the author of *Thomas Hardy in Our Time* (1995) and *The Word from Below: Essays on Modern Literature and Culture* (1987). In the excerpt below from his article, "Hardy: Versions of Pastoral," Langbaum discusses the novel as "Hardy's greatest nature poem" in which the landscape plays the definitive role in bestowing identity upon its inhabitants.]

The Return of the Native is Hardy's greatest nature poem. Hardy achieves the imaginative freedom and intensity of great poetry by daring to make the heath the novel's central character, the all-encompassing identity from which the human characters derive the individualities that emerge from the pass back into the heath. Hardy ties his characters to the heath by means of a device which is most conspicuous in *Far from the Madding Crowd* and *The Return of the Native:* characters appear for the first time as distant shapes on the heath, mysterious archetypes, taking on individualizing lineaments as they approach the observer. Hardy sometimes renews a character's identity by reintroducing him or her in this manner, making the observer (the technique requires an observer) rerecognize the character as if for the first time.

Thus Eustacia, after the opening chapter's powerful description of the heath at nightfall, appears to the observer as a landscape object. The reddleman watches the "form" of an old man (Eustacia's grandfather) "as it diminished to a speck on the road and became absorbed in the thickening films of night." He then looks upward toward a distant hill with a barrow (a prehistoric burial mound) upon it, and becomes aware that the barrow's summit

> was surmounted by something higher. It rose from the semi-globular mound like a spike from a helmet. . . . There the form stood, motionless as the hill beneath. . . . The form was so much like an organic part of the entire motionless structure that to see it move would have impressed the mind as a strange phenomenon.

"Strange" in the manner of Wordsworth's old leech-gatherer (probably in Hardy's mind) who, in his stillness breaks upon the observer as a huge stone that can only have moved there supernaturally. Only when Hardy's "form" moves can it be distinguished from the heath as a woman's figure, which turns out many pages later to be Eustacia. Instead of just evolving from the landscape, as in Wordsworth, Eustacia evolves from the heath through association with a primitive artifact and Guy Fawkes bonfires both of which descend from ancient Celtic culture. Hardy adds to Wordsworth an anthropological view of man's relation to landscape through organically evolved culture.

In *The Return of the Native* Hardy goes beyond Wordsworth in attempting to portray the heath as totally objective, beyond human categories of understanding. Insofar as the heath is comprehensible at all, it is comprehensible through contradictory aspects both deriving from and not deriving from human observation. This despite Hardy's usual practice as described in his journal entry of 23 August 1865: "The poetry of a scene varies with the minds of the perceivers. Indeed, it does not lie in the scene at all." Hardy's art is not so far as is generally thought from that of his contemporary, Henry James; the difference is that Hardy employs many points of view instead of one—almost all his important actions are carefully framed by observers, sometimes animal observers. The heath is unusual because not presented through points of view. Yet in this exceptional instance and others there remains the sense that the landscape or animals (the animals in the dicing scene, for example) are objectively there whether observed or not and that the full intensity of their being exceeds human observation. ⟨. . .⟩

Because his presentation is exceptional, Hardy's opening description of the heath at twilight exemplifies the aesthetic of the sublime, given the heath's affinity to night and its slightly threatening aspect:

> [T]he heath wore the appearance of an instalment of night which had taken up its place before its astronomical hour was come. . . . [A]t this transitional point of its nightly roll into darkness the great and particular glory of the Egdon waste began. . . . It could best be felt when it could not clearly be seen.

Hardy goes on to distinguish between the sublime and the beautiful in the manner of Burke's *The Sublime and the Beautiful* (1756). Its nocturnal and threatening qualities, says Hardy, "lent to this heath a sublimity in which spots renowned for beauty of the accepted kind are utterly wanting" (I, i, 2–3). The difference is that Burke treats the sublime as an alternative aesthetic; whereas Hardy treats it as antiaesthetic, as emphatically the taste for the nonbeautiful of modern reflective men who through science know the bleak truth about nature. These modern men, we learn when Clym is described, cannot themselves be beautiful because their faces are ravaged by thought and unpalatable knowledge. The modern taste for the antiaesthetic sublime becomes the post-Darwinian way of relating to nature. "I feel that Nature is played out as a Beauty, but not as a Mystery," Hardy wrote in his diary for January 1887 (*Life,* 185). With the current revival of interest in the sublime, Hardy's revision of Burke should be especially relevant.

The heath is presented as a particular place but also as the whole earth in "its nightly roll into darkness." In *The Return of the Native,* Hardy goes beyond Wordsworth in portraying the landscape as a total environment. The characters move on the heath as fish swim through the sea; the characters are brushed by the grasses they push through, they are observed uncomprehendingly by animals. "Tall ferns buried [Eustacia] in their leafage whenever her path lay through them, which now formed miniature forests, though not one stem of them would remain to bud the next year"—the last clause will apply also to Eustacia (IV, iii, 202). And of Clym we are told:

> The ferns, among which he had lain in comfort yesterday, were dripping moisture from every frond, wetting his legs through as he brushed past; and the fur of the rabbits leaping before him was clotted into dark locks by the same watery surrounding. (III, vi, 165–66) ⟨. . .⟩

The characters' total immersion in nature suggests pastoralism, and indeed *The Return of the Native* brings to a climax the series of pastoral novels beginning with *Under the Greenwood Tree* (1872). But *Return of the Native* is also the first of the great tragic novels constituting Hardy's major period. In making the transition to tragedy, *Return of the Native* seriously modifies pastoral which does not traditionally mix with tragedy. Hardy makes them mix by deepening the psychology to a point usually inappropriate to pastoral, and by taking a Darwinian view so that the nature which totally embraces the characters does not know them. The lovely sentence about miller-moths just precedes Clym's discovery of his mother dying on the heath of a snake bite.

—Robert Langbaum, "Hardy: Versions of Pastoral," *Victorian Literature and Culture*, vol. 20 (1993): pp. 245–47.

CHARLES E. MAY ON THE MAGIC OF METAPHOR

[Charles E. May is the author of *The Short Story: The Reality of Artifice* (1995) and *Edgar Allan Poe: A Study of the Short Fiction* (1991). In the excerpt below from his article, "The Magic of Metaphor in *The Return of the Native*," May focuses on the character of Eustacia Vye as evidence that this work can be read as a combination of two genres, as both romance and novel, through the metaphor of the witch.]

Critical controversy about nineteenth-century fiction has often centered on the generic question of whether a given work is to be read as a novel or a romance: This has especially been the case in the past twenty years since Northrop Frye not only warned us that in reading fiction we must begin by establishing a work's genre but also suggested a theoretical distinction between these two fictional forms based on the concept of characterization. Frye postulated that the difference between the two forms springs from the fact that the novelist deals with personality, "with characters wearing their *personae* or social masks," whereas the romancer does not attempt to create real people so much as "stylized figures which expand into psychological archetypes."[1]

Although Frye warned that pure examples of either the novel or romance were not to be found, that prose forms were always mixed like racial strains in human beings, his theory established no way to read works as actual mixtures of the two forms—only a way to read works as either one form or the other. "There is hardly any modern romance," Frye said, "that could not be made out to be a novel, and vice versa."[2] Consequently, critics have approached nineteenth-century fictional characters as either psychologically-motivated real people acting within a novelistic social similitude or as mythically-motivated archetypes acting within a psychologized allegorical code. Heathcliff and Lord Jim are only two of the more obvious examples. Characters in the works of Charlotte Brontë, Dickens and Hardy have also been treated thus alternatively. (As an aside here, the relevance of which will become apparent later, psychoanalytic criticism is similarly divided between those critics who analyze fictional characters as if they were real people on the therapeutic couch and those who interpret fictional characters as if they were embodiments of concepts in the Freudian metapsychology.)

Such an either/or approach to a mixed genre is a reductive use of theory and does little to further the study of genre as a guideline to interpretation. I think the issue deserves another look. While I will retain Frye's discriminants of psychological character versus psychological archetype, I hope to find a mediating principle between the two to show how a fictional figure in a "modern romance" can be read as both at once rather than one to the exclusion of the other. ⟨. . .⟩

Although Hardy's concern with the synthesis of novel and romance can be seen in all of his fiction, and consequently all of his major works have been interpreted as either one or the other, *The Return of the Native* seems to be the source of more disagreement and bafflement than the rest. The work has been variously called tragedy, parody, myth, social realism, and antichristian document. Eustacia Vye is one of Hardy's most puzzling creations, whose curiously bifurcated nature always seems to evade critical efforts to characterize her. One critic says her story is both myth and case history; another calls her both tragic heroine and parody of a heroine. Furthermore, many other elements in the work have been more quarreled about than clarified. Egdon Heath has been alternatively interpreted as hard physical reality and as purely symbolic device; the accidents and coincidences that dominate the plot have been called both the fault of weaknesses in the characters and the result of Hardy's philosophic determinism; the framework of magic and superstition that surrounds and infuses the action of the work has been termed both grotesque parody and animistic gratuitousness. ⟨...⟩

This combination seems most effectively achieved when a psychologically real character's obsession is so extreme that he or she projects the obsession on someone or something outside the self and then, forgetting that the source of the obsession is within, acts as if it were without. Thus, although the obsessive action takes place within a similitude of a realistic world, once the character has projected something inside outwards and then has reacted to the projection as if it were outside, this very reaction transforms the character into a parabolic rather than a realistic figure. Ahab, Gatsby, Heathcliff, Kurtz come to mind as examples.

The best place to begin this consideration of how these processes change Eustacia from psychological character to psychological archetype is at her death, when at the moment she plunges into the pool Susan Nunsuch fashions an image of her, sticks it full of pins and destroys it in the flames. Ruth Firor, in her study of Hardy's use of folklore, says "even the most casual reader cannot escape the feeling that . . . [Susan Nunsuch's] image is partly responsible for Eustacia's death."[7] However, since we cannot account for this responsibility psychologically (for Eustacia does not know of Susan Nunsuch's actions), nor can we explain it supernaturally (for this would violate the naturalistic plot of the story), we must account for it metaphorically. Since Eustacia is referred to as a witch throughout the story, both literally by the folk and figuratively by Clym, we could say that Eustacia the witch metaphorically destroys herself by means of the witch-like sympathetic magic of Susan Nunsuch's destruction of her image. This would be an unjustified metaphoric interpretation, were it not prepared for psychologically by Eustacia's repetitive compulsion to project her image and her actions on the external world.

Hardy makes this clear when Eustacia tries to excuse her action after she has turned Mrs. Yeobright away from her door: "instead of blaming herself for the issue she laid the fault upon the shoulders of some indistinct colossal Prince of the World, who had framed her situation and ruled her lot."[8] The last words we hear from her as she stands on the heath, "a perfect harmony," Hardy says, "between the chaos of her mind and the chaos of the world without," are: "How I have tried and tried to be a splendid woman, and how destiny has been against me! . . . I do not deserve my lot! . . . I was capable of much; but I have been injured and blighted and crushed by things beyond my control!" (p. 422).

Eustacia is one of those people Freud describes who "all their lives, repeat to their own detriment, the same reactions without any correction, or who seem to be dogged by a relentless ill-fortune." A closer inspection, Freud says, "shows they are unwittingly bringing ill fortune upon themselves. Thus we explain what is called a 'dae-monic' character as being due to the repetition compulsion."[9]

Notes

1. *Anatomy of Criticism: Four Essays* (New York: Atheneum, 1969), p. 304.

2. *Anatomy of Criticism*, p. 305.

7. *Folkways in Thomas Hardy* (Philadelphia: Univ. of Pennsylvania Press, 1931), p. 90.

8. Thomas Hardy, *The Return of the Native* (London: Macmillan, 1964), p. 353. Subsequent references to this, the Greenwood Edition of Hardy's novels, will follow the quotation in the text.

9. *New Introductory Lectures on Psycho-Analysis*, trans. W. J. H. Sprott (New York: W. W. Norton, 1933), p. 146.

—Charles E. May, "The Magic of Metaphor in *The Return of the Native*," *Colby Library Quarterly* 22, no. 2 (June 1986): pp. 111–12, 114–15.

[Perry Meisel is the author of *The Myth of the Modern: A Study in British Literature and Criticism After 1850* (1987) and *The Absent Father: Virginia Woolf and Walter Pater* (1980). In the excerpt below from the chapter entitled "*The Return of the Native*," Meisel discusses the "journey into the self," and the importance of landscape in defining personality.]

The apparently Darwinian asides in Knight's cliff adventure and at moments in *Far From the Madding Crowd* seemed designed to give expression to a scientific view of nature, assigning an external determinism to a universe that encompasses both the individual and the community. But, as we have seen in Darwin, such a view simply upholds the illusions of a myopic rationalism that refuses to examine its own perceiving lens. By the time he wrote *The Return of the Native,* Hardy seems to have been forced to tackle the initial conflict—between intellect and desire, rational, urban individual and rural community—by reassessing his entire imaginative perspective. The journey into the self has begun: the lens itself must be scrutinized. The question of method becomes correspondingly problematic as the irony of the book, that a native of Wessex has become the rationalist, suggests the involution that is underway. ⟨. . .⟩

Here, he places responsibility directly with his characters, invoking no determinism from without—the implication is, instead, that whatever determinants exist within a narrative are "by reason of the characters [themselves] taking no trouble to ward off the disastrous events produced"; what happens to them is a function of their own constitutions. By the "advantages of the letter-system" of storytelling, he seems to reaffirm our understanding of the poetics of the early novels: that the world of a novel becomes alive only when events become important to the characters and, as a result, affect the community in which they move. ⟨. . .⟩

His concern with the relation between landscape and the human figure assumes a form which reveals the needs that have wrought refinements in his poetics. The meaning of his earlier remark now becomes even more significant: "The writer's problem is, how to strike a balance between the uncommon and the ordinary . . . [while] . . . human nature must never be made abnormal. . . . The uncommonness must be in the events, not in the characters." At the same time, "[t]ragedy . . . should arise from the gradual closing in of a situation that comes of ordinary human passions" and ordinary human weaknesses in response to those passions. But Hardy stresses, too, that the "poetry of a scene varies with the minds of the perceivers." Thus landscape, in the sense of the relation between external scenery or objects and human figures, becomes the most natural mode for mediating the demands of his poetics. The "beauty of association" can be used as a means of defining character and event from a character's perspective. Even with some intellectual awareness of these possibilities, though, Hardy still uses landscape in only a limited way at this point in his career: as a reflection, by simile or analogy, of his characters' moods and natures. As his substantive concerns move away from a community-oriented perspective (where individuals are seen in terms of a society, as either members or intruders) toward the perspective of the individual himself, his imaginative methods become correspondingly refined. Hardy's changing use of landscape is important both as a mediator between human community and nature and as a means of creating individual consciousness. *The Return of the Native* furnishes the richest example of this brooding transitional period, as the universe of the early novels moves toward the vision of the later Hardy. ⟨. . .⟩

> In fact, precisely at this transitional point of its nightly roll into darkness the great and particular glory of the Egdon waste began, and nobody could be said to understand the heath who had not been there at such a time. It could best be felt when it could not clearly be seen . . . then, and only then, did it tell its true tale . . . the sombre stretch of rounds and hollows seemed to rise and meet the evening gloom in pure sympathy, the heath exhaling darkness as rapidly as the heavens precipitated it. And so the obscurity in the air and the obscurity in the land closed together in a black fraternization toward which each advanced half-way. [pp. 3–4] ⟨. . .⟩

In *The Return of the Native*, Hardy's landscape becomes personalized to a much greater degree than at any point in his earlier novels. And, as if to substantiate the feeling that the heath itself represents the explicit description of the psyche Proust was to achieve, the artist tells us that "[h]aggard Egdon appealed to a subtler and scarcer instinct, to a more recently learnt emotion, than that which responds to the sort of beauty called charming and fair" (p. 5). The separation between the perceiver and scene, of course, still remains; but an affinity between the perceptive sensibility and the nature of the world it beholds is clearly suggested. Hardy's early diary entry has already suggested this tendency: "The poetry of a scene varies with the minds of the perceivers. Indeed, it does not lie in the scene at all"; "the beauty of association" that he notes at the time of his completion of the novel confirms the fact that he was also moving consciously in this direction. The passage in the novel to which he refers in the note takes on added meaning in the context of the landscape:

> human souls may find themselves in closer and closer harmony with external things wearing a somberness distasteful to our race when it was young. The time seems near, if it has not actually arrived, when the chastened sublimity of a moor, a sea, or a mountain, will be all of nature that is absolutely in keeping with the moods of the more thinking among mankind. And ultimately, to the commonest tourist, spots like Iceland may become what the vineyards and myrtle-gardens of South Europe are to him now; and Heidelberg and Baden be passed unheeded as he hastens from the Alps to the sand-dunes of Scheveningen. [p. 5]

—Perry Meisel, *Thomas Hardy: The Return of the Repressed* (New Haven and London: Yale University Press, 1973): pp. 68–74.

ROBERT SQUILLACE ON HARDY AND THE MUMMERS

[Robert Squillace is the author of *Modernism, Modernity and Arnold Bennett* (1997). In the excerpt below from his article, "Hardy's Mummers," Squillace argues against other critics by maintaining that Hardy did not possess knowledge of the true pagan origins of mummers.]

⟨. . .⟩ Critics have consistently misinterpreted the meaning of the mummers' play Hardy depicts in *The Return of the Native* by crediting him with knowledge about the pagan origins of mumming that he almost certainly did not possess. At the root of this error is a tendency to attribute a modern sensibility to premodern writers; in fact, Hardy's true perspective on such folk practices as mumming was distinctly antimodern. Whereas such twentieth-century authors as T. S. Eliot, D. H. Lawrence, and W. H. Auden believed folk rites embodied profoundly current psychological truths, for Hardy such rituals represented an earlier stage in human development no longer accessible to contemporary man.

The history of mummers' plays is today a matter of general scholarly agreement.[2] The plays originated in a pagan ritual, performed around the time of the winter solstice, in which a god-personification of either the year or the sun was symbolically killed and resurrected to ensure fertility in the spring. During the Christian Middle Ages the ritual evolved into a Christmas ceremony, the events of the crusades and the legends of St. George infiltrating the ancient form. Depictions of individual combat between Christian and Saracen generally replaced the ritual action of killing the old year; all the dead knights on both sides were resurrected at the play's end by a comic doctor. St. George anachronistically appears as the chief crusading knight in the plays, probably because the most widespread versions of his life detail his murder and resurrection in Egypt. When printing became cheap enough to reach the rural poor, who maintained the mummers' play long after it lost fashion at court in the sixteenth century, such popularizations of Christian legends as the "The Seven Champions of Christendom" influenced mumming. Eventually, historical events of local importance entered many of the plays; thus communities along the southern coast of England often replaced Beelzebub with Buonaparte and St. George with King George, while Oliver Cromwell wandered into Irish versions. Also, the amount of slapstick humor in the plays increased over the centuries.

Ruth A. Firor's book, *Folkways in Thomas Hardy*, still the standard work on Hardy's use of folk materials, intimates that Hardy took conscious advantage of the play's pagan origins. After she describes the ancient ceremonies in detail, she writes, "On the whole, the mummers' play in *The Return of the Native* is considerably closer to the primitive source of folk-drama, we may safely believe, than the majority of extant folk-plays."[3] James Gindin's essay on Hardy's use of folklore in *The Return of the Native* follows Firor's reading. Gindin strongly implies that Hardy knowingly evoked the ceremony's original form: "The mummers' play in *The Return of the Native*, appropriately for the novel, is somber and traditional, the age old assurance that the good and life triumph finally over evil and death."[4] John Paterson, who has written extensively on the novel, goes even further in basing his reading of the play on its supposed evocation of the pagan ceremony. He writes that its "Christian veneer scarcely conceals its pre-Christian character as fertility rite celebrating the death of the year and its resurrection in the spring."[5] These interpretations all implicitly ascribe to Hardy the modernist method of using mythological or folk materials. That method is to ignore later accretions to the original tales or practices in order to penetrate to the truly primitive, which corresponds to the deepest reaches of the unconscious.

Critical unanimity, however, does not guarantee accuracy; the evidence that Hardy knew nothing about the connection between mumming and fertility rites is in fact overwhelming. ⟨...⟩

That Hardy says nothing in the novel itself to connect mumming with primitive rituals may be the strongest evidence that he did not know there was any such connection, for he rarely withholds information necessary for the reader's understanding. For example, he details the origins of the Guy Fawkes celebrations even though this information was readily available in such contemporary works as Brand's. Hardy writes: "Indeed, it is pretty well known that such blazes as this the heathmen were now enjoying are rather the lineal descendants from the jumbled Druidical rites and Saxon ceremonies than the invention of popular feeling about Gunpowder Plot."[14] Hardy almost certainly would not suppress important facts about the origins of mumming that would otherwise be unknown to his readers. Indeed, nothing in any of Hardy's personal writings, including the biography he wrote for Florence Hardy to publish as her own, even suggests that he knew the contemporary mis-identification of mumming with Saturnalia, made by such scholars as Strutt and Brand, before writing *The Return of the Native* (1878), though he would apparently read Udal's 1880 essay at some later time.[15] Although Hardy knew from observation a great deal about folk practices, he twice admitted to Udal (with whom he became acquainted in the 1880s): "I have never systematically studied Folk lore, nor collected dialect words. If I had done either I might have gained some valuable material in both kinds. I used in fiction such folklore as came into my mind casually, & the same with local words."[16] Thus, it seems unlikely that Hardy knew anything more specific about the origin of mumming plays than their obvious roots in medieval Christianity.

Notes

2. The following books give similar accounts of the pagan ceremonies from which mummers' plays originated and the subsequent accretion of other material: Alan Brody, *The English Mummers and their Plays* (Philadelphia: Univ. of Pennsylvania Press, 1969, 1970); Alex Helm, Norman Peacock, and E. C. Cawte, *English Ritual Drama* (London: Folk-Lore Society, 1967); R. J. E. Tiddy, *The Mummers' Play* (Oxford: Clarendon Press, 1923); E. K. Chambers, *The Mediaeval Stage*, 2 vols. (Oxford: Clarendon Press, 1933).

3. *Folkways in Thomas Hardy* (Philadelphia: Univ. of Pennsylvania Press, 1931), pp. 202–3.

4. "Hardy and Folklore," in *The Return of the Native*, by Thomas Hardy, ed. James Gindin, Norton Critical Edition (New York: Norton, 1969), p. 397.

5. "*The Return of the Native* as Antichristian Document," *Nineteenth-Century Fiction*, 14 (1959), 121–22.

14. *The Return of the Native*, Wessex ed. (London: Macmillan, 1912), p. 17; subsequent citations in the text are from this edition. For information about Guy Fawkes Day, see Brand, *Observations on Popular Antiquities*, pp. 205–16.

15. See Florence Emily Hardy, *The Early Life of Thomas Hardy, 1840–1891* (London: Macmillan, 1928) and *The Later Years of Thomas Hardy, 1892–1928* (London: Macmillan, 1930); *The Collected Letters of Thomas Hardy*, ed. Richard Little Purdy and Michael Millgate, 5 vols. (Oxford: Clarendon Press, 1978–85); Thomas Hardy, *Life and Art*, essays, notes, and letters collected by Ernest Brennecke, Jr. (New York: Greenberg, 1925); *The Personal Notebooks of Thomas Hardy*, ed. Richard H. Taylor (New York: Columbia Univ. Press, 1979); *The Literary Notebooks of Thomas Hardy*, ed. Lennart A. Björk, 2 vols. (New York: New York Univ. Press, 1985); and *Thomas Hardy's Personal Writings*, ed. Harold Orel (Lawrence: Univ. of Kansas Press, 1966). Hardy wrote to Udal in 1918: "I believe that you worked up the subject of Dorset mumming for the folk-lore Society" (*Letters*, V, 284).

16. *Letters*, V, 136; see also V, 111.

—Robert Squillace, "Hardy's Mummers," *Nineteenth-Century Literature* 41, no. 2 (September 1986): pp. 172–74, 177–78.

Plot Summary of
The Mayor of Casterbridge

Published in 1886 in two volumes, *The Mayor of Casterbridge* was first serialized in the *Graphic,* January–May 1886 and illustrated by Robert Barnes. At the time of its publication, critics did not appreciate how great a novel Hardy had written. *The Saturday Review* called it a disappointment while the *Spectator* complained of its "pagan reflections." Among the numerous literary influences on this novel, was Sophocles and the doctrine of learning through suffering. Many critics consider it to be Hardy's reworking of *Oedipus Rex,* with Michael Henchard resembling Oedipus, a man who tried unsuccessfully to avoid the consequences of a shameful deed. Furthermore, whereas Oedipus blinds himself and goes into voluntary exile, Henchard begins drinking, only to be lead out of the pub by his stepdaughter, walking "blankly, like a blind man." However, his stepdaughter does not share in his exile.

It is a late summer evening, "before the nineteenth century had reached one-third of its span," when Michael Henchard, a skilled laborer, "of fine figure, swarthy and stern in aspect," approaches the village of Weydon Priors, accompanied by a woman carrying a child. Nevertheless, though the couple walks together, upon closer scrutiny they are in fact very disconnected from each other. "[H]is taciturnity was unbroken, and the woman enjoyed no society whatever from his presence." It is Fair Day, September 15, and Michael Henchard soon becomes aggressively drunk on furmity (a milk drink) laced with rum, and sells his wife Susan and their daughter, Elizabeth-Jane for five guineas to a sailor, a stranger who enters upon the scene and whom we later learn was one Richard Newson. When Michael Henchard finally comes to his senses the following morning, and looks at the culpatory evidence of the sailor's bank-notes in his pocket, he also realizes the awful reality that he sold his family. He also remembers the sobering fact that his wife took this outrageous transaction literally as a binding contract and, without further ado, promptly left with her new "husband." Chapter II concludes with Michael Henchard vowing not to drink for the next twenty-one years and beginning a futile search for his wife and daughter, as the "weeks mounted up to months."

Some eighteen years later, we learn that Michael Henchard has prospered as a corn factor and has become the mayor of Caster-bridge." And it is at this time, [as described in chapter 3,] that Susan Newson and her daughter return from Canada to the fair grounds in search of Michael. Susan's marriage is over as her husband is thought to have died at sea. But, time has wrought many changes since mother and daughter were last at the fair grounds. "Certain mechanical improvements might have been noticed . . . machines for testing rustic strength and weight. . . . But the real business of the fair had considerably dwindled. The new periodical great markets . . . were beginning to interfere with the trade carried on here for centuries." They also encounter the furmity seller of eighteen years ago, who has now become an old woman on a very meager subsistence. Nevertheless, despite the passage of time and defining events that have shaped the destiny of the Henchard family, not least of which occurs when Susan soon learns that her first husband, Michael Henchard, has become the mayor of Casterbridge in addition to becoming a wealthy businessman. And, in furtherance of his success, Michael Henchard seeks a competent manager for his corn crop, news of which possible employment reaches a young Scotsman "of remarkably pleasant aspect," Donald Farfrae, who offers his managerial services.

Meanwhile, when Michael Henchard learns that Susan and Eliza-beth-Jane have returned, he devises an elaborate plan to court and "remarry" Susan, a plan which requires discretion given his political status. Henchard tells Susan to take a cottage in town and assume the name of her deceased husband, Newson, which gives Henchard the respectability and opportunity to court and finally remarry her, all the while believing Elizabeth-Jane to be his own daughter. Susan and Michael are soon remarried during a "Martinmas summer," an unusually warm autumn day in November. "He was as kind to her as a man, mayor, and churchwarden could possibly be." It is also during this time that Michael Henchard's relationship with Donald Farfrae starts to go sour. The two men have a falling out over one of the laborers, Abel Whittle, a "round shouldered, blinking young man" prone to oversleeping. Henchard feels compelled to yank Whittle out of bed one morning, consequently, angering Farfrae. A little further on, Henchard becomes jealous over Farfrae's popularity and reputation for exceptional business skills, which causes Henchard to dismiss his young manager. His dismissal is also very distressing to Elizabeth-Jane who has been attracted to him from the very start.

Donald Farfrae, however, turns his dismissal into an opportunity to go into business for himself, and becomes highly successful in his endeavor due to his amiable personality, which is in stark contrast to his former employer. "Character is Fate, said Novalis, and Farfrae's character was just the reverse of Henchard's, who . . . had quitted the ways of vulgar men without light to guide him on a better way."

Shortly after forfeiting Donald Farfrae's valuable assistance, Henchard faces yet another loss when Susan becomes seriously ill and dies. Interestingly, it is through Donald Farfrae's compassionate inquiry regarding Susan Henchard's health that the reader is told of her demise. "Some time later on Farfrae was passing Henchard's house. . . . He rang the bell so softly that it only sounded a single full note . . . and then he was informed that Mrs. Henchard was dead." While going through some of his wife's papers, Henchard comes across an envelope addressed to Elizabeth-Jane which is not to be opened till her daughter's wedding day. When Henchard decides to open it anyway, he makes the shocking discovery that Elizabeth-Jane is not, after all, his daughter, but Richard Newson's and, thus, his motivation for remarrying Susan for the sake of his daughter had now turned to "dust and ashes." In order to ascertain the truth of Susan's claim, Henchard observes the young woman while she is asleep. "In the present statuesque repose of the young girl's countenance Richard Newson's was unmistakably reflected." Henchard's attitude towards her hardens, and he begins to find fault with her manner of speaking and her willingness to do domestic work. In a word, she became an embarrassment to him in his elevated social status. "Convinced of the scathing damage to his local repute and position . . . Henchard showed a positive distaste for the presence of this girl not his own, whenever he encountered her." Nevertheless, unbeknownst to Henchard, Elizabeth-Jane embarks on a program of reading and writing and begins to study Latin. In the meantime, Michael Henchard's life and fortune continue to unravel when he learns that he has not been chosen to fill a vacancy as an alderman when his mayoralty ends. However, in yet another surprising reversal, while Henchard previously forbade Elizabeth-Jane to see Donald Farfrae when he believed her to be his legitimate daughter, he now sees the union of these two young people as a way of terminating any responsibilities he may have for her.

The situation for Michael Henchard becomes bleaker when a woman from the island of Jersey, Lucetta Templeman, with whom he had an affair during the years of his self-imposed estrangement from Susan, inherits property nearby Casterbridge and takes Elizabeth-Jane into her household. This newest liaison is the result of Lucetta's chance meeting of Elizabeth-Jane at the gravesite of Susan Henchard, at which time Lucetta offers her a job as a housekeeper and companion in her new residence, High-Place Hall. Ironically, while visiting her new residence before her actual employment, Elizabeth-Jane does not notice Michael Henchard's presence. Lucetta, on the other hand, goes out of her way to make her presence know to Henchard, explaining that her engagement of his daughter would now provide a convenient and respectable reason for his calling on his former lover. Henchard, for his part, is enticed by the fact that Lucetta had become a woman of means. "He was getting on towards the dead level of middle age, when material things increasingly possess the mind." But, instead of Henchard to whom Lucetta had written requesting a meeting, she finally receives a surprise visitor, Mr. Donald Farfrae, who has come to call on Elizabeth-Jane. Elizabeth-Jane is not home. She has been sent on a mission to bring Henchard to High-Place Hall and her absence allows Farfrae an introduction to Lucetta. Lucetta immediately becomes infatuated with him, and given Henchard's absence all these years, "[h]er heart longed for some ark into which it could fly and be at rest." Lucetta now desires Farfrae, whom she will eventually marry.

During this time, Henchard's situation continues to deteriorate with yet another mistake in judgment when he hires Jopp, the man who had originally applied for Farfrae's job. As it turns out, Jopp gives Henchard very bad counsel when he advises his boss to use every means possible to destroy Donald Farfrae. Furthermore, after consulting a local weather diviner, a very unreliable source of information, Henchard buys a surplus of grain, banking on a bad harvest driving up the price of corn. In keeping with other false illusions, the weather changes from bleak to favorable. "The temperament of the welkin passed from the phlegmatic to the sanguine; an excellent harvest was almost a certainty; and as a consequence prices rushed down." Added to this, is the public awareness of Henchard's sexual indiscretions as his past comes back to taunt him. At one point, Henchard is required to preside in the trial of an old woman at the Petty Sessions (a local court dealing with minor offenses); the old furmity seller, who is accused of creating an obscene nuisance, speaks out about an incident twenty years ago and, thus, exposes Henchard's original wife sale, completing his public disgrace. Added to this exposure of Henchard's sexual indiscretions is Jopp's (who has now been fired from his managerial position) treachery. Having come from Jersey himself, Jopp knew that Henchard once courted Lucetta Templeman at an inn, named Peter's Finger, a place of ill repute, "where waifs and strays of all sorts loitered about." It is here that Jopp, seeking revenge against Lucetta for not helping him to get a job with Farfrae, decides to read the contents of a package of love letters; these disclose the truth about Lucetta and Henchard's past relationship. The gossip is now "spreading like a miasmatic fog through Mixen Lane, and thence up the back streets of Caster-bridge," while the patrons of Peter's Finger decide that a "skimmity ride," a parade of the lower classes consisting of effigies and rough music with the purpose of mocking adulterous behavior or spousal misconduct, was entirely in order. The resulting humiliation is over-whelming for Lucetta and it soon kills her.

By now Henchard is now both bankrupt and drunk, his twenty-one years of vowing not to touch a drop of liquor are up. Captain Newson now returns, causing Henchard's face and eyes to appear to die at the sound of his name. Henchard, fearful of losing Eliza-beth-Jane, lies to Newson tells him that both Susan and his daughter are dead. "Towards the young woman herself [Hen-chard's] affection grew more jealously strong with each new hazard to which his claim to her was exposed." Nevertheless, although it appears to Henchard that Newson has accepted the news of his daughter's decease, the sailor persists in his search and is even-tually reconciled to his daughter. Farfrae, who is now the Mayor of Casterbridge, marries Elizabeth-Jane, while Henchard leaves Casterbridge, "discarding for ever the shabby-genteel suit of cloth and rusty silk hat that since his decline had characterized him in the Casterbridge street, thereby ending his life in the same circum-stances in which he began—as a poor, itinerant journeyman labourer." Henchard dies in solitude in a hovel on Egdon Heath, attended only by the humblest and simplest of his former workmen. His final wishes are found written on a piece of paper pinned to the head of his bed, "[t]hat Elizabeth-Jane Farfrae be not told of my death, or made to grieve on account of me." ❀

List of Characters in
The Mayor of Casterbridge

Michael Henchard – As the novel's protagonist, Henchard is the "man of character," the mayor to whom the title refers. When the narrative begins, Henchard is an unhappy twenty-one year old hay trusser. In a drunken rage he sells his wife and daughter at a county fair. Eighteen years later, Henchard's fortunes have risen and he has become both the mayor and most successful corn merchant in the town of Caster-bridge. But the crimes of his youth return when his wife, Susan, appears with her daughter, Elizabeth-Jane. Henchard's fortune begins to plummet as he loses everything and everyone he cared about.

Susan Henchard – An unassuming woman, married to Michael Hen-chard when the novel opens. When her drunken husband sells her at a country fair to a sailor, Susan believes the contract to be binding and goes off to live with him until he is supposedly lost at sea. Assuming he is dead, she and her daughter, Elizabeth-Jane return to the English countryside in search of Henchard. When she finds him, Susan agrees to remarry thereby allowing him to make amends for past wrongs.

Elizabeth-Jane – The daughter of Susan Henchard and Newson. She bears the same name as the child born to Susan and Michael Hen-chard, who actually died shortly after Michael sold the pair. Upon arriving in Casterbridge, her mother keeps the details of Elizabeth-Jane's life a secret. When the truth of her paternity comes to light, how-ever, she is cruelly rebuffed by Henchard. By the time Henchard is ready to be reconciled with her, it is too late, for Newson has returned.

Donald Farfrae – The Scotsman who arrives in Casterbridge at the same time as Susan Henchard and Elizabeth-Jane, Farfrae impresses Michael Henchard with his knowledge of the corn trade. He agrees to stay on in the town as the mayor's business manager and revolution-izes the way corn trading is handled in Casterbridge. His efficiency and good humor make him very popular among the town's citizens. Although the young man becomes Henchard's adversary, he remains fair-minded and patient in his dealings with the fallen man.

Lucetta Templeman – The woman whom Michael Henchard meets, courts and proposes to marry. Their plans are ruined, however, when

Susan Henchard unexpectedly returns with her daughter. Upon hearing of Susan Henchard's death and having inherited a large sum of money, Lucetta eventually moves to Casterbridge with the expectation of rekindling her affair with Henchard. However, she falls in love and marries Donald Farfrae. When her past liaison with Henchard is discovered and publicly mocked, Lucetta becomes seriously ill and dies.

Newson – The sailor who buys Susan and her daughter from Michael Henchard.

Joshua Jopp – The man Henchard intends to hire as his assistant before meeting Farfrae. When Jopp shows up late for his appointment, Henchard tells him that he has already hired Farfrae though Henchard will later hire Jopp after Farfrae starts his own business. Nevertheless, Jopp betrays Henchard when asked to deliver a packet of love letters to Lucetta. Jopp gets sidetracked to Peter's Finger, the inn on Mixen Lane, and his reading of the love letters to the unsavory clientele eventually leads to the "skimmity-ride" that causes Lucetta's death.

Abel Whittle – One of the workers, he is also the source of the first disagreement between Henchard and Farfrae, as Farfrae thinks that Henchard is too rough with Whittle when he is constantly late for work. In the end, he is the sole caretaker of Michael Henchard during his final days on Egdon Heath.

Benjamin Grower – One of Henchard's creditors, Henchard asks Lucetta to tell him that they will soon be married as an excuse for delaying payment on his debts. She is unable to do so, because Grower was one of the witnesses to her secret marriage to Farfrae. During the skimmity-ride, Grower tries unsuccessfully to apprehend those responsible.

Christopher Coney – A peasant in Casterbridge. He digs up the body of Susan Henchard and steals the coins used to weigh down her eyes.

Nance Mockridge – A peasant who, after being insulted by Henchard, divulges that Elizabeth-Jane once acted as a servant in the Three Mariners Inn. Nance also participates in planning the skimmity-ride.

Mother Cuxsom – A peasant in Casterbridge.

Solomon Longways – A peasant in Casterbridge. ✿

Critical Views on
The Mayor of Casterbridge

PETER J. CASAGRANDE ON THE ARCHITECTURAL MATRIX

[Peter J. Casagrande is the author of *Hardy's Influence on the Modern Novel* (1987) and *Tess of the d'Urbervilles: Unorthodox Beauty* (1992). In the excerpt below from his section entitled "The Architectural Matrix of *The Mayor of Casterbridge*," Casagrande discusses some of the symbolic meaning in Hardy's use of architectural detail.]

The Architectural Matrix of *The Mayor of Casterbridge*

In *The Mayor of Casterbridge,* published some three years after *Two on a Tower,* Hardy seems to be mediating between the views of redemption he exhibited in *The Trumpet-Major, A Laodicean* and *Two on a Tower.* In setting for a time the old-fashioned Henchard and the reforming Farfrae side by side as friends and partners in the grain trade, Hardy flirted with the strategy of Somerset in *A Laodicean* to juxtapose an old, ruinous building and a new one. It might even be argued that *The Mayor,* in its pervasive use of some of the old buildings of Dorchester, memorializes and thus symbolically preserves Henchard and the old order, Casterbridge functioning in this in much the way Overcombe Mill functions in *The Trumpet-Major.* On the other hand, in showing Henchard's gradual displacement by Farfrae, Hardy seems to be repeating the view in *Two on a Tower* that the old must give way to the new—theology to science, Speer to observatory, Viviette to Tabitha. If in *The Mayor* Hardy flirts with each of these views but embraces none of them, it is because in each of them he had averted tragedy. In the three novels that precede *The Mayor,* the amending and restoring powers of intelligence, charity and self-sacrifice are actively in play; the idea that change is decay seems to have been set aside. In *The Mayor,* however—in its conception of character as fate, in its fatalistic turn of plot; in its peculiar use of architectural setting—intelligence and love are found, finally, to be inadequate to the task of redemption or restoration. A deterioristic view of things prevails.

This—that restoration or redemption is impossible—is the tragedy, and Hardy is in full possession of his tragic concept in *The Mayor*. But at the same time he was incapable of displaying it without qualifying it, without expressing his anguish that it should be true that all is decay. And so the tragic vision in *The Mayor* contends with an antiquarian and commemorating attitude in the novel, an attitude that urges that if restoration is impossible it is yet powerfully appealing, an authentic and profound human need. In making this observation it is worth noting that Hardy wrote *The Mayor* during a flurry of architectural and antiquarian activity between 1880 and 1886. This included not only his writing three 'architectural' novels, but his joining the Society for the Protection of Ancient Buildings and the Dorset Natural History and Antiquarian Field Club, as well as his designing and building Max Gate. *The Mayor* is an intensely local novel at the same time that it is a tragedy of universal scope and significance. Henchard is associated with Faust, with Cain and with Saul; but important aspects of his character derive as well from 'local' personalities of Dorchester-past—not just a man who sold his wife, but also, as I shall show, from a Dorchester stonemason who refused to take part in the razing of a fine old Dorchester house called the Trenchard Mansion.

It might be said that in *The Mayor* Hardy's attitude toward Henchard and the old order he represents is deeply divided between an antiquarian and an aesthetic aim. On the one hand he is trying to memorialize old Dorchester (Casterbridge), to recall and thus preserve the picturesqueness and bustle of a county town before the intrusion of the railway, farm machines, and a new style of life. On the other, he is dedicated to showing, in all the beauty of its grim truth, the working of the law of decay, both in Henchard, whose defects of character are irremediable, and in the historical process itself, which replaces a Henchard with a Farfrae with ruthless inexorability. This latter impulse—to show the beauty of decay—Hardy would call 'the artist instinct'; the former—to preserve the beauty of former things—he would call 'the caretaking instinct'. Both phrases occur in a striking passage in 'Memories of Church Restoration', in which the dilemma of the Hardy who reluctantly and almost guiltily restored old churches can be seen to be much the same as that of the creator of the incorrigible but powerfully attractive Michael Henchard of *The Mayor*:

The artist instinct and the care-taking instinct part company over the disappearing creation [i.e. the ruinous church]. The true architect, who is first of all an artist and not an antiquary, is naturally most influenced by the aesthetic sense, his desire being, like Nature's, to retain, recover, or recreate the idea which has become damaged, without much concern about the associations of the material that idea may have been displayed in. Few occupations are more pleasant than that of endeavouring to recapture an old design from the elusive hand of annihilation. Thus if the architect have also an antiquarian bias he is pulled in two directions—in the one by his wish to hand on or to modify the abstract form, in the other by his reverence for the antiquity of its embodiment. . . . In short, the opposing tendencies excited in an architect by the distracting situation can find no satisfactory reconciliation. All that he can do is of the nature of compromise.

In *The Mayor,* Hardy, as 'artist', tries to exhibit the working of the inexorable process that annihilates both churches and men; this is 'the idea that has become damaged', the law of decay that has been obscured by belief in various redemptive schemes, whether human or divine. At the same time, as 'antiquary', he seeks to commemorate the 'embodiments' of the tragic truth, 'the [human] associations of the material' in which the tragic idea found expression. In short, in *The Mayor* Hardy is a tragic artist with an 'antiquarian bias', a novelist torn between his obligation to show the deterioristic working of history, of circumstances, and of character and his duty to memorialize the victims of this, for him, fatal process.

—Peter J. Casagrande, *Unity in Hardy's Novels: 'Repetitive Symmetries.'* (Lawrence, Kansas: The Regents Press of Kansas, 1982): pp. 183–85.

R. P. DRAPER ON OEDIPUS AND FATE

[R. P. Draper is the editor of *The Literature of Region and Nation* (1989) and co-author of *An Annotated Critical Bibliography of Thomas Hardy* (1989). In the excerpt from his article, "*The Mayor of Casterbridge,*" Draper discusses some aspects of Michael Henchard's character within a literary/historical tradition.]

The sub-title of *The Mayor of Casterbridge* reads, 'a story of a man of character', and in his Preface Hardy declares that it is 'more particularly a study of one man's deeds and character than, perhaps, any other of those included in my Exhibition of Wessex life' (33). Henchard is the dominant character; no other figure in the novel approaches him in stature, and no other receives the same amount of attention, either in terms of space devoted to his doings or in fullness of characterisation. He thus occupies the centre of the stage very much as a figure in classical tragedy does, and he has consequently been regarded, by D. A. Dike, for example, as 'a modern Oedipus', and by John Paterson as a figure subject to the same retribution as Oedipus or Lear for an act (in Henchard's case the selling of his wife) which constitutes 'the violation of a moral scheme more than human in its implications'.

Oedipus cannot escape his fate. His arrogance may contribute to his undoing, but irrespective of his character, his tragedy is predetermined by the will of the gods. Henchard's tragedy, however, is more evidently the product of his character. When the business rivalry between Henchard and Farfrae begins to gather momentum, and Farfrae shows signs of prospering like Jacob in Padan-Aram, the narrator first offers alternative explanations of Farfrae's success in terms of 'his northern energy' or 'sheer luck', but immediately corrects himself with the comment: 'But most probably luck had little to do with it, Character is Fate, said Novalis, and Farfrae's character was just the reverse of Henchard's, who might not inaptly be described as Faust has been described—as a vehement gloomy being who had quitted the ways of vulgar men, without light to guide him on a better way' (143). Not only Henchard's business ventures, but his separation from his wife and child, his sudden liking for Farfrae, his sense of the conflicting demands of moral duty and mayoral dignity in his response to Susan's reappearance, his blowing hot, cold and then hot again in his relations with Elizabeth-Jane, his jealousy over Lucetta, his increasing paranoia with regard to Farfrae—all the major developments in his life are influenced by his possessive, impulsive, domineering, yet generous character. Nevertheless, he can be regarded as a hero in the classical, Aristotelian mode in that he is neither so good as to seem undeserving of his downfall, nor so bad as to forfeit the reader's sympathy; and though, as befits a Victorian novel, the strengths and weaknesses of his character engage our attention to a much greater extent than is ever the case with the protagonist in Greek tragedy (and even more than is the case with most Shakespearean heroes), his character is defined, again in the classical manner, through its expression in action. He is known by his utterances and deeds; they are the man's character in motion.

But as with all Hardy's novels, character is not exclusively fate. Chance, or coincidence, also plays a significant part in determining the form of action in which character can express itself. Thus, Henchard's native impetuosity accounts for his taking such a sudden liking to Farfrae, but it is chance which brings the latter to Casterbridge just at the moment when Henchard needs a manager; and it is chance, operating almost as a malign fate, which causes Henchard to learn that Elizabeth-Jane is not his real daughter at the very moment when he has persuaded her to take his name. In this novel, as compared with *Tess of the d'Urbervilles* or *Jude the Obscure,* such things are not unduly prominent. Perhaps the one sequence which strikes the reader as too obviously contrived is that which occurs in chapters 21–3. Elizabeth-Jane goes to stay at High-Place Hall because Lucetta thinks this will be a convenient way of bringing Henchard to her house, but he decides to teach her a lesson by taking his time. Lucetta interprets this as a result of his dislike for the girl and begins to think of Elizabeth-Jane as more of a hindrance than a help to her plan. She therefore arranges to get Elizabeth-Jane out of the house one morning and writes a note inviting Henchard for that particular time. It is Farfrae who arrives first, however, coming with the intention of wooing Elizabeth-Jane, but ending by being fascinated with Lucetta herself. Here it is the needs of the plot which are uppermost. Hardy is faced with the problem of grafting the new Lucetta material, and the sexual rivalry which will spring up in consequence between Henchard and Farfrae, on to their existing commercial rivalry. The narrative manipulation by which he seeks to do it is skilful enough, but it is achieved at the cost of making the characters' movements seem contrived, or, at best, puppet-like responses to the promptings of a mocking fate. To that extent it detracts from the overall impression of the novel as 'a story of a man of character'—though it is still character which makes the ironic events strike deep instead of being brushed aside as mere temporary misunderstandings. In general, however, the balance between character and chance is well maintained, and Henchard's downfall is felt as something to which he himself has very largely contributed. When he leaves Casterbridge a disgraced figure he acknowledges the justice of events with a stoical self-awareness: 'I—Cain—go alone as I deserve—an outcast and a vagabond. But my punishment is *not* greater than I can bear!' (334). It is the character of the man which prompts his self-destructive actions, and in these words he declares an acceptance of those actions which gives him tragic status of an existential kind. Character is the source both of his undoing and of the strength he finds to endure the affliction it brings.

To many readers it may seem—as, indeed, Hardy wishes it to seem—that Henchard's punishment does not fit his crime; but the emotional attitude embodied in his self-critical formula remains entirely appropriate. King Lear's self-pity which makes him cry out that he is a man more sinned against than sinning would not do if it were to come from Henchard's lips, though, as Robert C. Schweik argues, towards the end of the novel there are changes in tone and atmosphere and in the burden of the narrator's philosophical reflectiveness which do prompt a different judgement from the one Henchard makes on himself. If the Henchard of the latter part of the novel still seems culpable, particularly in his lies to Newson about Elizabeth-Jane, that offence is not on the scale of his original wife-selling.

—R. P. Draper, "*The Mayor of Casterbridge,*" *Critical Quarterly* 25, no. 1 (Spring 1983): pp. 57–59.

D. H. Fussell on Changing Times

[D. H. Fussell has held the position of Lecturer in English and Drama at Loughborough University of Technology. In the excerpt below from his article, "The Maladroit Delay: The Changing Times in Hardy's *The Mayor of Casterbridge*," Fussell discusses some of the complex meanings in Hardy's notion of mistiming.]

Enough that in the present case, as in millions, it was not two halves of a perfect whole that confronted each other at the perfect moment; a missing counterpart wandered independently about the earth waiting in cross obtuseness till the late time came. Out of which maladroit delay sprang anxieties, disappointments, shocks, catastrophes, and passing-strange destinies.

'The maladroit delay' which Hardy describes ⟨in *Tess of the d'Urbervilles*⟩ as being the source of Tess's and men's distress is a term which is particularly rich in suggestion and carries important significance in relation to his earlier novel, *The Mayor of Casterbridge*. Both novels portray a series of mistimings of a variety of kinds and the discords which arise from them. In this article I propose to outline this variety in *The Mayor of Casterbridge* and to consider in particular Hardy's sense of time.

One of the central themes of Hardy's works, and one which has received a considerable amount of critical attention, is change: 'flux and reflux—the rhythm of change—alternate[s] and persist[s] in everything under the sky' (*Tess*, p. 399). It is a sense of change which is caught so vividly and subtly in the poem 'During wind and rain'. The title suggests both enduring and being at the centre of the experience of change—'during' suggests much of the character of *The Mayor of Casterbridge*, and indeed many of the other novels. *The Mayor of Casterbridge*, like the poem, is about families; it begins with a picture of a family characteristically moving along a road and with the figures of the parents prophetically divided from each other. The novel is preoccupied with a sense of the complicated pressures which exist in or are brought to bear on the family; and this is a theme which will be increasingly developed in *Tess of the Durbervilles* and *Jude the Obscure*, an interest, as Raymond Williams says, in 'what happened to people and to families in the interaction between general forces and personal histories'. Directly related to this is the implication of the title of the novel itself, *The Life and Death of the Mayor of Casterbridge*. If Tess and Jude give their names to the novels, Michael Henchard gives his public title: the novel is very much to do with public order and the public place and the maladroit connections or disconnections with the personal worlds of the characters. Hardy perhaps draws attention to his concern to catch the authenticity of these two orders, the personal and the public or external world of reality, in his comment on the signpost over the Three Mariners:

Hereon the Mariners, who had been represented by the artist as persons of two dimensions only—in other words, flat as a shadow—were standing in a row in paralysed attitudes. Being on the sunny side of the street the three comrades had suffered largely from warping, splitting, fading and shrinkage, so that they were but a half invisible film upon the reality of the grain, and knots and nails which composed the signboard. As a matter of fact, this state of things was not so much owing to Stannidge the landlord's neglect, as from the lack of a painter in Casterbridge who would undertake to reproduce the features of men so traditional.

The passage is characteristic of Hardy in that the details of his scenes have the capacity to evoke larger meanings, meanings which often have the quality of suggestion rather than the absolute stability of a definition. Here there is, I think, a criticism of the way in which art has reduced the human complexity of the ordinary man to a frozen stereotype, ignoring the full dimension of his being. And the reason why this emasculation of a particular class of person continues lies in the fact that no artist has emerged who has been either sufficiently interested or sufficiently capable to do such persons justice. The figures in the inn sign, moreover, are apparently painted not on a background but placed on the surface of the wood—this background with its grain, knots and nails, its design, is substantially of the actual world, a world composed out of nature and shaped by the craft of man. The suggestion is, therefore, that the sign or the novel requires a proper synthesis of the complex portrayal of individual character and the appropriately structured background of actuality; and that actuality *is* structured, by the shapes in the substance of the material itself, the grain and the knots, and by the nails, the fixing pins of the craftsman/artist. In this passage, then, I think that Hardy is reflecting on the condition of the English novel and indicating his idea of his own art; he recognises his need to give full dimension and shape to the individual life of his characters and to maintain the reality of the actual world in or against which they are placed. At the same time, the final words perhaps mark Hardy's awareness of the importance of his role as a provincial novelist.

Thus although the idea of seasonal change as expressed in 'During wind and rain' remains very important in the novel, it exists more in the background, underlying events; at the front there is a complex and inter-related portrayal of the dimensions, the causes and effects of change of a private and public kind, and a gathering of 'impressions', both of which are the product of Hardy's sustained and sensitive, contemplation of the spectacle he creates.

The pattern of change in the novel is traced not exclusively but most dramatically in the public life of the central character; the life and death of Michael Henchard; and it is placed against the rise of Donald Farfrae, a man who, as Henchard had been eighteen years earlier, is on his way: 'I am on my way to Bristol—from there to the other side of the warrld, to try my fortune in the great wheat-growing districts of the West' (p. 77).

The irony is that his energies focus themselves not in the New World but in the old world of Wessex. But this is not simply to say that the conflict between the two men, the one from the south-west, the other from afar, is a conflict between the native and the outsider: to see the novel as representing the destruction of a rural world with values which are held to be admirable by the outside world of rational and scientific advancement is, as many critics have said, naive. In fact, to be accurate, all of the central characters of the novel are outsiders to Casterbridge, for the town is as an economic centre possessed of a cosmopolitan nature and I shall look at this point in more detail in a moment. It would be more truthful to say that Casterbridge and indeed its Mayor are in a condition which needs and gives opportunity to such a character as Farfrae's, as in fact was the case eighteen years earlier for Henchard himself. If Farfrae ultimately contributes to Henchard's downfall whilst contributing positively to the economic and working order of the place, it is partly because there is something in the cornfactor, in his feelings as a man, that prevents him adjusting his personal affairs so that his business affairs may survive. He is unwilling and unable to engage in that kind of diplomacy so that, for example, he chooses to prevent the relationship between Elizabeth-Jane and Farfrae from developing. The relationship might have been of commercial benefit but it is offensive to him as a person. Thus the rise and fall of Henchard juxtaposed to and related to the rise of Farfrae is one indication of the complex theme of change.

—D. H. Fussell, "The Maladroit Delay: The Changing Times in Hardy's *The Mayor of Casterbridge*," *Critical Quarterly* 21, no. 3 (Autumn 1979): pp. 17–19.

[Robert C. Schweik is the editor of *Far from the Madding Crowd: An Authoritative Text, Backgrounds and Criticism* (1986) and co-author of *Reference Sources in English and American Literature: An Annotated Bibliography* (1977). In the excerpt below from his article, "Character and Fate in Hardy's *The Mayor of Casterbridge*," Schweik discusses some of the inconsistencies in the novel as impressionistic style of writing.]

Perhaps the most compelling evidence of really fundamental inconsistencies in *The Mayor of Casterbridge* is to be found, not in those analyses intended to show that the novel is seriously flawed,[1] but in the startlingly divergent interpretations proposed by critics who have attempted to discover some underlying consistency in Hardy's treatment of the relationship of Henchard's character to his fate. Two recent discussions of *The Mayor of Casterbridge* exemplify the almost polar extremes to which this divergence can tend: as John Paterson has interpreted the novel, Henchard is a man guilty of having violated a moral order in the world and thus brings upon himself a retribution for his crime; but, on the other hand, as *The Mayor of Casterbridge* has been explicated by Frederick Karl, Henchard is an essentially good man who is destroyed by the chance forces of a morally indifferent world upon which he has obsessively attempted to impose his will.[2] The fact is that *The Mayor of Casterbridge* is capable of supporting a variety of such conflicting assessments both of Henchard's character and of the world he inhabits, and further discussion of the novel must proceed, I think, by giving this fact more serious attention. Hardy strenuously insisted that both as novelist and as poet he dealt with "impressions" and made no attempt at complete consistency;[3] what is worth considering is whether or not Hardy put his inconsistency to any use and what, if any, advantage he may have gained by doing so.

The sacrifice of simple consistency in fiction can yield some important compensations, particularly in the freedom it allows a novelist to manipulate detail and aspect as a means of controlling and shifting reader attitude as the work progresses. It is possible to make a rhetorical use of elements whose implications will not add up to a logically consistent whole. Clearly such a rhetoric can serve the imaginative purpose of the novel if it is arranged to generate an initial image of life which is then altered by subsequent changes in the handling of character and event, and when the progress of the whole is such as to move the reader from one way of looking at things to another less immediately acceptable view of them. ⟨. . .⟩

The largest elements in *The Mayor of Casterbridge* are four relatively self-contained and structurally similar "movements" of progressively diminishing lengths, roughly comprising chapters i–xxxi, xxxi–xl, xli–xliii, and xliv–xlv. Each provides a variation on a common pattern: an initial situation which seems to offer some hope for Henchard is followed by events which create doubt, fear, and anxious anticipation for an outcome that comes, finally, as a catastrophe. Furthermore, in each of these succeeding movements there is a reduction in the scope of Henchard's expectations and a corresponding increase in the emphasis which Hardy puts both upon Henchard's anxiety for success and upon the acuteness of his subsequent feeling of failure. Much of our response to Hardy's account of Henchard's final withdrawal and lonely death depends, certainly, upon the cumulative impact of these successively foreshortened and intensified movements from hope to catastrophe; but the particular tragic response which *The Mayor of Casterbridge* seems calculated to evoke is also the product of other adjustments in detail and emphasis from movement to movement which have the effect of repeatedly shifting our perception of Henchard's character, of the kind of world he inhabits, and of the meaning of the catastrophes which he suffers.

The first and by far the longest of these movements (slightly more than half of the novel) falls into two almost equal parts. The opening fourteen chapters of *The Mayor of Casterbridge* establish a situation which seems to offer hope for Henchard's success. Following the brief prefatory account of Henchard's economic and moral nadir at Weydon Priors and his resolution to make a "start in a new direction,"[4] Hardy abruptly bridges an intervening eighteen years to reveal the outcome of Henchard's vow; and not only does Henchard reappear transformed into a figure of affluence and social standing, but events now seem to augur his further financial and social success: he gains the commercial support and personal companionship of Farfrae, effects a reconciliation with his lost wife and child, and seems about to find a solution to the awkward aftermath of his affair with

Lucetta. Hardy implies, certainly, that Henchard has undergone no equivalent moral transformation; we learn that he is conscientiously abstemious, but is otherwise simply "matured in shape, stiffened in line, exaggerated in traits; disciplined, thought-marked—in a word, older," and what details contribute to our first impression of the new Henchard—his aloofness, his harsh laugh, the hint of moral callousness in his stiff reply to complaints about his bad wheat—tend to support, as Hardy remarks,

> conjectures of a temperament which would have no pity for weakness, but would be ready to yield ungrudging admiration to greatness and strength. Its producer's personal goodness, if he had any, would be of a very fitful cast—an occasional almost oppressive generosity rather than a mild and constant kindness (v).

Notes

1. See, for example, James R. Baker, "Thematic Ambiguity in *The Mayor of Casterbridge*," *Twentieth Century Literature*, I (April, 1955), 13–16; Robert B. Heilman, "Hardy's 'Mayor' and the Problem of Intention," *Criticism*, V (Summer, 1963), 199–213.

2. John Paterson "*The Mayor of Casterbridge* as Tragedy," *Victorian Studies*, III (Dec., 1959), 151–172; and Frederick R. Karl, "*The Mayor of Casterbridge*: A New Fiction Defined," *Modern Fiction Studies*, VI (Autumn, 1960), 195–213.

3. *The Works of Thomas Hardy*, Wessex Edition (London, 1912), I, xii and xviii.

4. *Works*, Wessex Edition, V, ch. ii. All further citations are to this edition and are indicated by chapter numbers inserted parenthetically in the text.

> —Robert C. Schweik, "Character and Fate in Hardy's *The Mayor of Casterbridge*," *Nineteenth Century Fiction* 21, no. 3 (December 1966): pp. 249–51.

MICHAEL TAFT ON FOLKLORE AND THE LITERARY IMAGINATION

[Michael Taft is an editor of *The Centennial Index: One Hundred Years of the Journal of American Folklore* (1988) and *Blues Lyric Poetry: An Anthology* (1983). In the excerpt below from his article, "Hardy's Manipulation of Folklore and Literary Imagination: The Case of the Wife-Sale in *The*

Mayor of Casterbridge," Taft discusses the wife-sale in terms
of Hardy's thorough knowledge of local traditions.]

That Hardy used folklore in his writings in a very conscious manner
is beyond dispute. A great many scholars have pointed out this fact,
and indeed a favorite pastime of some Hardy critics involves listing
all the various traditions which Hardy called upon in his works. But
these catalogues of traditional tales, ballads, customs, and beliefs,
although valid enough, do little to increase our understanding of
exactly how Hardy used his knowledge of local traditions to aid his
writing, how the folklore of his region inspired his talents, or how
Hardy managed to combine the raw material of collected traditions
with the ideas and visions of his imagination.

Although Hardy used folklore quite consciously, he never
intended to write ethnographies, nor was he methodical or scientific
in his observations of the folklore around him. Lombardi describes
the casual nature of Hardy's methodology:

> The lore which Hardy uses in his Wessex novels was col-
> lected in a rather haphazard way. He recorded snatches of
> songs in his notebooks, beliefs and remedies on the back
> of old envelopes, paying no attention whatsoever to his
> informant. . . . This is no unusual revelation about
> Thomas Hardy, for he was so at home in the Wessex
> region that his imagination was free to work upon mate-
> rial thoroughly familiar to him for a lifetime.

This methodology, or lack thereof, sets Hardy apart from the
many county collectors who were his contemporaries in rural England, and indeed he seems to have had little to do with the Folk-Lore
Society which, since 1878, had been the leading organization
devoted to serious folklore scholarship in Britain. Hardy's "amateur
status" in the field of folklore was probably for the best, since it pre-
vented him from becoming ensnared in the theoretical and method-
ological traps of nineteenth-century folklore scholarship. His
intuitive, subjective manner of collecting folklore and his ability to
recombine traditional material and to mingle folkloric facts with the
products of his imagination may have been bad ethnography, but
was excellent literature.

Hardy's manipulation of traditional material is perhaps no better
seen than in the opening chapter of *The Mayor of Casterbridge.* The

young Michael Henchard, depressed by his inability to find work and oppressed by the responsibilities of looking after a wife and young child, becomes intoxicated on furmity laced with rum. In this drunken state, he offers to auction his wife to the highest bidder among his fellow drinkers. Though his offer is, at first, only half serious, the outcome is the first in a series of Henchard's self-inflicted tragedies. A sailor buys Henchard's wife and immediately disappears with her and the child. The next morning, a remorseful Henchard seeks his wife, although his effort is less than whole-hearted, but neither his wife and child nor the sailor can be found.

In his preface to the novel, Hardy refers to this incident as one of the major events in the story; indeed, it is the central incident, for all other events in the novel either grow out of the wife-sale or are greatly affected by it. The entire novel is a series of consequences, all resulting from Henchard's auction of his wife.

It is impossible to know with certainty what inspired Hardy to write *The Mayor of Casterbridge,* but it seems likely that his knowledge of wife-sales kindled his imagination. But what are the sources of Hardy's information on wife-sales? The wife-sale or auction, although not an everyday occurrence in nineteenth-century England, was one of those incidents which would occur from time to time and would appear in local newspapers as a commentary on the perverse or bizarre nature of country folk. Social historians have documented many cases, extending from the turn of the eighteenth century to the first decades of the twentieth century.

Hardy himself read back issues from local newspapers and among the news items which he copied into his *Facts Notebook* was the following typical piece on wife-sales:

> *Sale of a Wife.* Man at Brighton led a tidy looking young woman up to one of the stalls in the market with a halter round her neck and offered her for sale. A purchaser was soon found, who bought her for 30 s/—which he paid, and went off with his bargain amid the sneers and laughter of the mob, but not before the transaction was regularly entered by the clerk of the market book and the price of 1 shilling paid. He also paid 1 s/—for the halter, and another 1 s/ to the man who performed the office of auctioneer. We understand that they were country people and that the woman had 2 children by her husband, one of whom he

consents to keep and the other he throws in as a makeweight to the bargain.

This item would seem to answer the question of Hardy's source for the opening of *The Mayor of Casterbridge,* but this was not the only wife-sale story which Hardy knew, nor does the opening chapter entirely conform in detail to this newspaper account. Indeed, in a letter which Hardy wrote to Howard Temperly in January of 1924, he admits that no one wife-sale story conforms in every respect to the one in his novel.

Hardy was undoubtedly aware of many newspaper accounts of wife-sales. Beyond this source, he had probably heard local gossip from time to time about other such occurrences. But a third major source for Hardy was the popular ballad tradition, of which he was very much aware. Hardy was a keen observer of musical traditions, as he was of all folk traditions. Whether he heard singers recounting the news of a wife-sale or whether he read broadside ballads of such events, Hardy undoubtedly made note of these poetic accounts for his future novel. Indeed, there were many broadsides about wife-sales circulating in England in the nineteenth century. Although some were in prose form, most accounts were in the traditional form of the topical ballad, and such songs became incorporated into the repertoires of local singers.

—Michael Taft, "Hardy's Manipulation of Folklore and Literary Imagination: The Case of the Wife-Sale in *The Mayor of Casterbridge,*" *Studies in the Novel* 13, no. 4 (Winter 1981): pp. 399–401.

Plot Summary of
Tess of the d'Urbervilles

Published in 1891, *Tess of the d'Urbervilles* was serialized in watered-down form in the *Graphic,* from July–December 1891. It is a Wessex novel, set in the south of England, sometime during the late 1800s. Subtitled "A Pure Woman," *Tess of the d'Urbervilles* tells the tragic life story of a peasant girl, Tess Durbeyfield, who ends up on the scaffold. In his preface, Hardy addresses the critical response to the tragic fate of his protagonist. "That these impressions have been condemned as 'pessimistic'—as if that were a very wicked adjective—shows a curious muddle-mindedness. It must be obvious that there is a higher characteristic of philosophy than pessimism, ... which is truth."

As **Phase the First: The Maiden** opens, we are introduced to the Durbeyfield family. John Durbeyfield, on the way home from a day's work as a "haggler" (a pedlar), encounters Parson Tringham, who relates to Mr. Durbeyfield that he is in fact descended from the once famous d'Urbervilles, a descendant of an "ancient and knightly family" who date back to the time of William the Conqueror in 1066. Unfortunately, however, as the parson explains, the "D'Urberville" family have long since ceased to exist. "At Kingsbere-sub-Greenhill: rows and rows of you in vaults, with your effigies, under Purbeck-marble canopies." Neverthelss, John Durbeyfield adopts a superior attitude as he encounters a stranger walking along the road. "There's not a man in the county' South-Wessex that's got grander and nobler skillentons in his family than I." But, when John Durbeyfield finally reaches home, he learns that an unfortunate accident has taken place. The Durbeyfield horse, Prince, has accidentally, and as it will turn out prophetically, been killed by a mail cart due to the negligence of Tess and her brother Abraham. When John Durbeyfield responds by telling his wife, Joan, of their wealthy relatives, she is immediately seized with the idea that Tess, their eldest daughter, should call upon her relatives, to "claim kin," as a means of alleviating their impoverished condition. "Do you know there's a very rich Mrs. D'Urberville living on the outskirts o' the Chase. . . ? You must go to her and claim kin, and ask for some help in our trouble." Though Tess initially objects to such a venture, she is also feeling very guilty and, thus, acquiesces to this stratagem of securing either money or work from her cousins, the d'Urbervilles. When

Tess arrives at The Slopes, she notices that the d'Urberville estate is far from staid and established, but surprisingly contemporary. "It was a recent erection, indeed almost new, and of the same rich red color that formed such a contrast with the evergreens of the lodge." As it turns out, the estate belongs to the misplaced "Stoke-D'Urbervilles," "a somewhat unusual family to find in such an old-fashioned part of the country." She meets Alec d'Urberville, a man with "touches of barbarism in his contours," who immediately finds himself attracted to her and he arranges for Tess to become the caretaker for his blind mother's poultry. "The community of fowls to which Tess had been appointed as supervisor, purveyor, nurse, surgeon and friend, made its headquarters in an old thatched cottage standing in an enclosure . . . [which] was now a trampled and sanded square." Once she is installed at the d'Urberville residence, her cousin Alec takes her on a wild carriage ride, the purpose of which is to frighten and thereby gain control over her, but Tess successfully resists his advances. But, at the close of Phase the First, Alec finally succeeds. Finding Tess alone and asleep in the Woods, he rapes his young cousin. "Why was it that upon this beautiful feminine tissue, sensitive as gossamer, and practically blank as snow as yet, there should have been traced such a coarse pattern as it was doomed to receive . . . many thousands of years of analytical philosophy have failed to explain to our sense of order."

In **Phase the Second: A Maiden No More,** (12–15) Tess must now live with the consequences of Alec's violation. It is now October, four months after her arrival, when Tess sets out to return home. "[I]t was terribly beautiful to Tess to-day, for since her eyes last fell upon it she had learnt that the serpent hisses where the sweet birds sing. . . ." Alec makes an unsuccessful bid for her forgiveness, stating that he is "ready to pay to the uttermost farthing." Tess deserts Alec along the road and soon encounters a sign painter, "an artizan of some sort," whose signs preach against vice and sin. "Thy, Damnation, Slumbereth, Not. 2 Pet. ii 3," which message, "against the peaceful landscape . . . [in] vermillion words shone forth." When Tess finally confronts her mother with the rape and asks why she did not warn Tess about the dangers of "men-folk," Mrs. Durbeyfield clings to the same ignorant and misguided belief that Tess should have compelled Alec to marry her for her own good and the benefit of the impoverished Durbeyfields. By now, Tess has fallen into abject misery and become the focal point of village gossip, finding no consolation in either her friends or attendance at church services. "The bedroom she shared with some of the children formed her retreat more continually than ever. . . . So close kept she that at length almost everybody thought she had gone away." The following August finds Tess working in the fields while taking breaks to feed her unbaptized baby. When the baby falls ill, she baptizes the child herself, appropriately naming him Sorrow, and shortly thereafter she must bury her infant son in a nearly forgotten part of a graveyard. "So the baby was carried in a small deal box . . . and buried by lantern-light . . . in that shabby corner of God's allotment where He lets the nettles grow. . . ." By the end of this second phase, Tess resolves to re-enter the world and seek employment suitable to her social status. "She would be dairymaid Tess, and nothing more."

In **Phase the Third: The Rally,** a few months following this tragedy, Tess begins working at the Talbothays Dairy, owned by the kindly Richard Crick. Her spirits now being lifted by the beautiful countryside, Tess is very happy to be in new surroundings. "Either the change in the quality of the air from heavy to light, or the sense of being amid new scenes where there were no invidious eyes upon her, sent up her spirits wonderfully." It is here that Tess meets Angel Clare, a young man of twenty-six years and the son of a local parson, who aspires to own a farm in either England or one of the colonies, rather than be a minister as his father expects. Though he is working as a novice dairy-farmer at Talbothays, there is that about him which suggests "something educated, reserved, subtle, sad, differing." Furthermore, he is remotely familiar to Tess. A loving relationship between Angel and Tess begins to evolve. "Every day, every hour brought to him one more little stroke of her nature, and to her one more of his. Tess was trying to lead a repressed life, but she little divined the strength of her own vitality." In the meantime, there is a crisis at the dairy when the milk does not begin to turn to butter, and a superstitious tale goes around that this is surely a sign that somebody at the dairy is in love. Eventually, however, the butter begins to form and tranquility is restored, while one of the milk-maids, Retty Priddle, observes that Angel is in love with Tess. In the meantime, Angel has been observing Tess, waiting for the right moment to profess his love for her. However, Tess is convinced that a relationship with a man of his social status could never last, and thus she resists him. Nevertheless, despite her instincts about the success of such a union, Tess will eventually marry Angel Clare in the fourth phase. And that possibility is implied in the narrator's final comment at the close of this third part. "A veil had been whisked aside; the tract of each one's outlook was to have a new horizon thenceforward—for a short time or long."

Phase the Fourth: The Consequence begins with Angel persuading his family that Tess, a woman who understands the responsibilities of farm life is a far more suitable marital choice for him, rather than the "good and devout" Mercy Chant, the young woman whom his parents had intended him to marry. Angel finally prevails over his parents' reluctant willingness to meet Tess. "They said finally that it was better not to act in a hurry, but that they would not object to see her." It is at this time that Reverend Clare tells Angel about the recent transformation of Alec d'Urberville, an "upstart squire," who has become a lay minister and street preacher. Having prepared his family, Angel repairs to the dairy to ask Tess to become his wife. Once again, Tess protests, stating that she is not an "honourable woman," although she cannot bring herself to be specific, at first explaining that she does not want to marry, preferring to just love him instead and, when Angel persists, she gives the excuse that his parents would not approve of her humble background. Nevertheless, Angel prevails. "His experience of women was great enough for him to be aware that the negative often meant nothing more than the preface to the affirmative. . . ." Angel also now learns from Tess that she is descended from the d'Urberville line, and, for practical reasons, suggests that she retain the ancient spelling of her family name. "'My mother, too, poor soul, will think so much better of you on account of it.'" Much relieved that she has told Angel of her d'Urberville connection, Tess looks forward to her marriage with joyous anticipation. "There was hardly a touch of earth in her love for Clare. To her sublime trustfulness he was all that goodness could be, knew all that a guide, philosopher, and friend should know." However, while on a shopping expedition with Angel, much to Tess's dismay she encounters two men from Alec d'Urberville's village of Trantridge who loudly proclaim that they know of her and her past. Angel confronts them and the two admit that they may be mistaken about Tess's identity, at which time Angel dismisses the entire incident. Though Tess wants Angel to know the truth before their marriage, the note she has slipped under his door gets caught in the carpet and remains undetected. Phase the Fourth ends with the traumatic events following the marriage ceremony as

Angel reminds Tess of their promise to each other to confess their past wrongdoing. Though Clare is safely able to reveal an earlier affair, an "eight-and-forty hours' dissipation with a stranger," the event that triggers the heartrending rupture in their marriage is Tess's confession of her past relationship with Alec d'Urberville, "murmuring the words without flinching, and with her eyelids drooping down."

Phase the Fifth: The Woman Pays begins with the aftermath of their confessions, as "the complexion even of external things seemed to suffer transmutation as her announcement progressed." While Tess forgives Angel for his past indiscretions, Angel cannot forgive Tess for having a child with another man. Indeed, so extreme and narrow-minded is his reaction that Angel declares Tess to be a different woman from the one he thought he was marrying. As a way for him to cope with the shocking news, Angel suggests that they cancel the marriage, as he is better able to love from afar. "'I think of people more kindly when I am away from them;' adding cynically, 'God knows; perhaps we shall shake down together some day, for weariness; thousands have done it!'" The end result is that Angel will go to Brazil for a year and Tess will go back home. Neither one of them fares very well from the separation. "Mentally she remained in utter stagnation," while Angel is "lying ill of fever in the clay lands near Curitiba in Brazil . . , in common with all the English farmers and farm labourers who, . . . were deluded into going thither by the promises of the Brazilian government. . . ." Tess eventually leaves home again for work in another town at Flintcomb-Ash farm, where the working conditions are very harsh. "The stubborn soil around her showed plainly enough that the kind of labour in demand here was of the roughest kind." However, Tess is reunited with some of her friends from Talbothays, and they all adjust to the routine of hard work. Tess is determined to see Angel's family in nearby Emminster, but loses her nerve at the last minute. "This self-effacement in both directions had been quite in consonance with her independent character of desiring nothing by way of favour or pity to which she was not entitled on a fair consideration of her deserts." On her return to Flintcomb, Tess sees Alec again, now a practicing evangelical minister, preaching to the folks in the countryside. While the congregation listens to his sermon, Tess is struck by the "strange enervating conviction that her seducer confronted her."

Phase the Sixth: The Convert begins with Tess's unhappiness at the change in Alec's appearance, from a man of wealth to that of a common person, with the strong implication that, from Tess's perspective, the newly-made Alec is a sham and his modified appearance merely cosmetic. "It was less a reform than a transfiguration. The former curves of sensuousness were now modulated to lines of devotional passion. The lip-shapes that had meant seductiveness were now made to express supplication. . . ." His circumstances greatly changed and his mother having passed away, Alec tells Tess the details of his conversion, a conversion for which the Reverend Clare is responsible. It is now that he finally hears what happened to Tess after she left him in the road the day she left Tantridge. With this new knowledge of their son and the hardships which befell Tess as a result of his raping her, Alec asks her to accompany him to Africa, as his wife, in order to do missionary work there. He implores Tess to marry him so that he can make amends to her and, by virtue of her consent, become "a self-respecting man" himself. A little further on, he is adamant that Angel has abandoned her and will never return. Nevertheless, his persuasive efforts notwithstanding, Tess writes an impassioned letter to Angel Clare, assuring him of her unending love. "Anyone who had been in a position to read between the lines would have seen that at the back of her great love was some monstrous fear, almost a desperation, as to some secret contingencies which were not disclosed." At the same time, Tess's sister, Liza Lu, comes to Flintcomb-Ash with news of their parents' failing health. When Tess arrives, she finds her mother recovering from her illness, while her father dies suddenly from an unknown ailment. And with his demise, the burden of the family's welfare falls on Tess's shoulders. Destitute and homeless, the Durbeyfields have nowhere to go. "To her, and her like, birth itself was an ordeal of degrading personal compulsion whose gratuitousness nothing in the result seemed to justify, and at best could only palliate." Tess thinks once again of Alec's money and the comforts her family can use. When she finally sets out to find him in church, she finds him in the astonishing position of lying atop a crypt, a "moving effigy" which, moments later, "leapt off the slab and supported her." At the same time, Marian and Izz, Tess's friends from Talbothays, write a letter to Angel imploring him to come home and rescue Tess. "Look to your Wife if you do love her as much as she do love you. For she is sore put to by an Enemy in the shape of a Friend."

Phase the Seventh: Fulfillment. In the meantime, Angel returns from Brazil to look for Tess and to begin his own farm in England. When Angel finds Tess's family, Joan informs him that Tess has gone to Sandbourne, a fashionable seaside resort in the south of England. Angel finds Tess there, and Tess asks him to leave and not return for her. But Angel is determined to stay for he has now been reconciled to the fact that he had judged Tess too harshly and returned too late. And as a further complication, Angel's return causes Tess to accuse Alec of lying to her when he insisted that she had been abandoned by her husband. Thus, in a fit of rage, Tess stabs Alec through the heart with a carving knife and kills him. Tess then finds Angel to tell him of the deed, and though he cannot believe it, he is overjoyed by her return. Nevertheless, despite Angel's disbelief, Tess has indeed committed a terrible crime and must flee the scene immediately before the authorities arrest her. She and Angel travel by the back roads with the intention of getting to a port and leaving the country as quickly as possible. They spend a week in a vacant house, observed only by the sympathetic caretaker, and thus are reunited in blissful seclusion for a short time. "The caretaker was so struck with their innocent appearance . . . that her first indignation at the effrontery of tramps and vagabonds gave way to momentary sentimentality over this genteel elopement, as it seemed." Nevertheless, they are soon discovered, their journey ending at Stonehenge, the ancient pagan monument. The police arrest Tess and take her away. In the final scene, just prior to her execution, Tess has Angel promise to marry her sister Liza Lu once she is gone. Angel agrees and he, alone with Liza Lu, witness a black flag raised in the city of Wintoncester, signifying that Tess's death sentence has been carried out. The two, Angel and Liza, leave together, and the tragic tale of Tess ends. "'Justice' was done, and the President of the Immortals (in Aeschylean phrase) had ended his sport with Tess. And the d'Urberville knights and dames slept on in their tombs unknowing." ✤

List of Characters in
Tess of the d'Urbervilles

Tess Durbeyfield – A beautiful, loyal young woman Tess is committed to her impoverished family who live in the village of Marlott. Her life is complicated when her father discovers he is descended from the noble line of the d'Urbervilles with Tess being sent to work at the d'Urberville mansion. Unfortunately, her ideals cannot prevent her from sliding further and further into misfortune after she becomes pregnant by Alec d'Urberville. The terrible irony is that Tess and her family are not really related to this branch of the d'Urbervilles at all because Alec's father, a merchant named Simon Stokes, simply assumed the name after he retired.

Angel Clare – An intelligent young man who has decided to become a farmer to preserve his intellectual freedom from the pressures of city life. Angel's father and his two brothers are respected clergymen, but Angel's religious doubts have kept him from joining the ministry. He meets Tess when she is a milkmaid at the Talbothays Dairy, and quickly falls in love with her.

Alec d'Urberville – The handsome, amoral and manipulative son of a wealthy merchant named Simon Stokes. Alec is not really a d'Urberville—his father simply took the name of the ancient noble family after he built his mansion and retired. Alec seduces the naïve and inexperienced Tess when she comes to work for his family. Though he later tries to make amends, it is hopeless, for Tess will never love him.

John Durbeyfield – Tess's father, a lazy peddler in Marlott, who seizes upon the idea that his connection with the noble line of the d'Urbervilles will prove to be easy and profitable.

Joan Durbeyfield – Tess's mother, has a strong sense of propriety and a very particular agenda for Tess. She is continually disappointed with the way things have worked out for her daughter. Given over to predictions and fortune telling, she attaches great credence to the Compleat Fortune-Teller, "an old thick volume . . . so worn by pocketing that the margins had reached the edge of the type." Nevertheless, she is forgiving, especially when she becomes completely dependent upon Tess.

Mrs. d'Urberville – Alec's mother, the widow of Simon Stokes, is blind and an invalid.

Marian, Izz Huett, and Retty Priddle – Milkmaids whom Tess befriends at the Talbothays Dairy, all of whom are in love with Angel. They take it hard when Angel chooses Tess over them. Nevertheless, they are devoted to Tess: Marian helps her find a job at a farm called Flintcomb-Ash, and she and Izz write Angel a plaintive letter encouraging him to give Tess another chance.

Reverend Clare – Angel's father, a somewhat intractable but principled clergyman in the town of Emminster. Mr. Clare considers it his duty to convert the populace; one of his most difficult cases proves to be none other than Alec d'Urberville.

Mrs. Clare – Angel's mother, a loving but somewhat snobbish woman who places great stock in social class.

Reverend Felix Clare – Angel's brother, a village curate.

Reverend Cuthbert Clare – Angel's brother, a classical scholar at Cambridge.

Eliza Louisa Durbeyfield – Tess's younger sister, she has all of her sister's good qualities and none of her bad ones. Before she is executed, Tess entrusts her sister to Angel's care.

Sorrow – Tess's son with Alec d'Urberville. Sorrow dies in his early infancy, after Tess christens him herself. She later buries him herself as well, and decorates his grave.

Mercy Chant – The daughter of a friend of the Reverend Clare. Mr. Clare hopes Angel will marry Mercy, but after Angel marries Tess, she is engaged to Cuthbert instead.

Richard Crick – A dairy farmer and the owner of Talbothays, he is very kind to Tess and Angel. ❀

Critical Views on
Tess of the d'Urbervilles

KRISTIN BRADY ON TESS AND ALEC

[Kristin Brady is the author of *The Short Stories of Thomas Hardy* (1982) and *George Eliot* (1992). In the excerpt below from her article, "Tess and Alec: Rape or Seduction?," Brady discusses the ambiguity of Alec's actions.]

From the time when *Tess of the d'Urbervilles* was first published in 1891, critical response has focused on the closeness of Hardy's narrator to his victimized protagonist, his tendency to act as her advocate and protector even as he subjects her to the terrible fate of his story. Hardy's own recognition of the advocate role is apparent in his notorious subtitle to the novel. 'A Pure Woman Faithfully Presented by Thomas Hardy', and the protective role is implicit in the epigraph from *Two Gentlemen of Verona*: '. . . Poor wounded name! My bosom as a bed shall lodge thee.' Hardy's defence of Tess, this suggests, will be that of a lover rather than of a legal representative. Hardy, in fact, confessed in a letter to Sir George Douglas that 'I . . . lost my heart to her as I went on with her history' and complained to Thomas Mac-Quoid that 'I have not been able to put on paper all that she is, or was, to me.' Hardy's sense of the incompleteness and inadequacy of the novel seems to have been acute. ⟨. . .⟩

⟨. . .⟩ Though these feelings of partial failure are by no means unique to Hardy, they seem to have a special application to his situation when writing *Tess of the d'Urbervilles,* a novel whose textual history reveals an unusually complex process of revision and rethinking. As much recent criticism has revealed, Hardy's original portrayal of Tess shows more physical familiarity between Tess and Alec before her loss of virginity in The Chase, while Hardy's own tendency toward partisanship, as well as his emphasis on Tess's victimization, increased in the later stages of the manuscript. These changes are no doubt linked to the difficulties Hardy encountered in trying to find a publisher for the novel's periodical publication. A general disinclination among editors to see female sexuality portrayed frankly, exemplified in Mowbray Morris's irritation at the novel's pervasive 'succulence', seems to have driven Hardy to de-emphasize Tess's sexual responses. By giving increased prominence in the later stages of the manuscript to the villainy of both Alec d'Urberville and Angel Clare, for example, Hardy was able half to suggest that Tess was more a passive victim of male aggression and idealization than an active participant in her own disastrous fate. Mary Jacobus argues that Hardy's original vision of Tess was falsified by the revisions: if Tess is simply a victim, then neither her sexuality nor her moral position in the novel is interesting.

⟨. . .⟩ What seems to some readers an unevenness or contradictoriness in the final version of the novel is in fact the natural result of the turbulent circumstances surrounding its composition and of its controversial subject matter: not simply seduction, but the sexual responses of a woman who became pregnant by a man she did not love and then recovered sufficiently to feel a strong attraction to another man.

Tess is not, indeed, the typical betrayed maiden, who either forsakes sexual relationships altogether in the aftermath of her moral lapse or pines away hopelessly for her seducer. Elizabeth Gaskell's Ruth, in contrast to Tess, devotes the rest of her life after her seduction to good works and to her son, while Beauty of 'Saturday Night in Arcady' (the seduction section of *Tess* that was published separately as a story) differs radically from the novel's heroine in her response to her seducer. Beauty implores him not to desert her and loses all of her former spirit and independence. Her fellow workers observe that 'to him she was deferential thenceforward, that she started when he came into the field and when he joked jokes of the most excruciating quality she laughed with a childlike belief in them'. Such a conclusion to the events at the haytrusser's and in The Chase seems startling to the reader who already knows the novel, for it is inconceivable that Tess would respond in such a way to Alec. What distinguishes her from other seduced maidens is also what makes her such a dangerous subject for fiction: that she could have sexual responses, though of varying intensities and kinds, to two different men.

One can never ignore altogether the serious restrictions on Hardy as he attempted to treat female sexuality in *Tess,* but it would also be simplistic to attribute all the novel's ambivalence to Mrs. Grundy. Much recent feminist criticism dwells on the extent to which Hardy's narrator seems himself to exhibit a fundamental ambivalence toward Tess's sexuality. The narrator's undeniably erotic fascination with her takes the form of a visual preoccupation with her physical presence, and it has even been suggested that the narrator derives an almost sadistic pleasure from Tess's suffering, that he shares in part the distorted views of her held by both Alec and Angel, and that he in some sense does himself violate her with his male voice and male eye. By the same token, the narrator seems to retreat from and close his eyes to the most explicit and direct manifestations of the sexuality which so fascinates him. As Penny Boumelha has perceptively remarked, Tess's sexuality is ultimately 'unknowable' and 'unrepresentable' by the narrator, and he withdraws completely from her consciousness at the most crucial points in her life: the moment when she was wakened to Alec's return in The Chase, the weeks following that scene when she was his mistress, the time of the discovery of her pregnancy and the birth of her child, the points when she decided to return to Alec and then to murder him and flee with Angel. Major events often take place between chapters and phases of the book, and are conveyed to the reader only by the narrator's factual reference to their having happened. Indeed, Tess's real thoughts and feelings are rarely presented in the novel, except when she suffers the consequences of her actions. Her moral choices seem obscured in ambivalence, while their results are vividly and dramatically portrayed. The effect of these constant jumps in the narration is that the reader can have a firm sense of Tess's suffering and her role as victim, but a somewhat confused sense of her own participation in her fate.

—Kristin Brady, "Tess and Alec: Rape or Seduction?," Thomas Hardy Annual, no. 4 (1986): pp. 127–30.

Mary Jacobus on Maternal Imagery

[Mary Jacobus is the author of *Psychoanalysis and the Scene of Reading* (1999) and *First Things: The Maternal Imaginary in Literature, Art and Psychoanalysis* (1995). In the excerpt below from her article, "Tess's Purity," Jacobus discusses issues of maternity in the novel.]

'Even imagination is the slave of stolid circumstance': Hardy's lament (in 'Candour in English Fiction', a symposium on the censorship question published by the *New Review* in January 1890) is a protest at the tyranny exercised over the novelist by the conditions of magazine publication. Designed for household reading, the family magazines necessarily failed (in Hardy's words) to 'foster the growth of the novel which reflects and reveals life'. In particular, a rigid set of taboos governed the fictional treatment of sexual questions—questions which were increasingly being debated elsewhere at the time, both in the novel itself and in the more progressive journals. Hardy's experience during the previous months in trying to publish *Tess of the d'Urbervilles* lies behind his impatience, and the compromises he was about to make must already have been in his mind. The acuteness of his sense of frustration and defeat in the face of the opposition encountered by *Tess* (and, later, by *Jude the Obscure*) is explicable partly in terms of the pain which these compromises caused him. 'Art', he noted in 1890, 'consists in so depicting the common events of life as to bring out the features which illustrate the author's idiosyncratic mode of regard'. With this emphasis on fidelity to a personal vision goes Hardy's belief in the autonomy of the novelist's imagination. 'Candour in English Fiction' speaks of situations as developing a life of their own; the 'faithful artist' must narrate what the logic of unfolding events dictates. To tamper with them is a form of artistic self-betrayal which strikes at the very basis of the novelist's commitment to his fictional world—at his own 'candour'. ⟨. . .⟩

In the autumn of 1889, three successive rejections of the half-completed *Tess* had shown Hardy the price he had to pay, if not for writing in the English language, at any rate for serial publication. ⟨. . .⟩

The form of Hardy's compromise is implicit in the novel's defiant subtitle, 'A Pure Woman'—added at the last moment, Hardy tells us, as 'the estimate left in a candid mind of the heroine's character—an estimate that nobody would be likely to dispute' (1912 Preface). In retrospect he clearly regretted the controversy aroused by his addition ('*Melius fuerat non scribere*. But there it stands'). The label caused trouble from the start. To those who accept a Christian definition of purity, it is preposterous, and to those who do not, irrelevant. The difficulty in both cases is the same—that of regarding Tess as somehow immune to the experiences she undergoes. To invoke purity in connection with a career that includes not simply seduction, but collapse into kept woman and murderess, taxes the linguistic resources of the most permissive conventional moralist; as the redoubtable Mrs. Oliphant put it, in a review which epitomizes the moral and critical opposition aroused by *Tess*, 'here the elaborate and indignant plea for Vice, that it is really Virtue, breaks down altogether'. On the other hand, to regard Tess as unimplicated is to deny her the right of participation in her own life. Robbed of responsibility, she is deprived of tragic status—reduced throughout to the victim she does indeed become. Worst of all, she is stripped of the sexual autonomy and that capacity for independent being and doing which are among the most remarkable features of Hardy's conception.

Hardy himself makes things worse by seeming to adopt the argument for a split between act and intention—Angel Clare comes to realize that 'The beauty of a character lay not in its achievements, but in its aims and impulses, the true record lay not among things done, but among things conceived' (f. 488, p. 388). Yet Angel's response to Tess at the end of the novel is remarkable because he no longer makes this distinction but—knowing her a murderess—accepts her as she is: 'Mortal, guilty, but to me / The entirely beautiful' (Auden, 'Lullaby', 11.9–10). Alternatively, it could be argued that the terminology of conventional Christian morality is being ironically misapplied to reveal its inadequacy and challenge the narrow Pauline definition of purity-as-abstinence originally held by Angel. But Hardy works best below the surface and his imagination is at its weakest when roused to argument. In this respect the novel's epigraph (from *Two Gentlemen of Verona*) is more helpful than its subtitle: 'Poor wounded name! My bosom as a bed / Shall lodge thee'. Hardy's compassionate identification with his heroine functions on a deeper and more intimate level than that of case-making. How often do we, not see, but feel her, sleeping or waking up, as Alec feels her damp cheek against his in the Chase, or Angel when she comes yawning downstairs at Talbothays, 'warm as a sunned cat' from lying down in her clothes (f. 240*, p. 210). We register all the more sensitively the rending of flesh that is so palpably present to us—whether metaphorically (the coarse pattern which Alec traces on her 'gossamer' tissue), or realistically (the stubble which makes her arm grow raw and bleed as she works on through the day in the harvest-field at Marlott). Such authorial allegiance to a living, breathing, sentient woman evades external standards of judgement or vindication altogether.

The need to make a special case for his heroine forced Hardy away from the simpler outline and different emphasis of his original conception. The main features of the Ur-*Tess* included Tess's seduction, the birth and death of Sorrow, and her courtship by Angel, breaking off with their marriage and his wedding-night confession. More baldly than the later version, the Ur-*Tess* dealt with the common enough situation of a country girl seduced by her employer on first going into service. Her social, economic, and sexual vulnerability are unequivocally defined. Tess's original name, 'Love' (modified successively to Cis, Sue, and Rose-Mary before emerging as Tess), suggests that Hardy always had in mind the crudely polarized attitudes to female sexuality embodied in Alec d'Urberville and Angel Clare (sexual possession versus idealization). But it is arguable that the oppositions were at this stage less clear-cut, more realistically blurred, and more humanely conceived, than they later became.

—Mary Jacobus, "Tess's Purity," *Essays in Criticism* 26, no. 4 (October 1976): pp. 318–21.

DALE KRAMER ON THE TRAGEDY OF CONSCIOUSNESS

[Dale Kramer is the editor of *The Cambridge Companion to Thomas Hardy* (1999) and editor of the Oxford University Press edition of *The Mayor of Casterbridge* (1987). In the excerpt below from the chapter entitled "*Tess of the D'Urbervilles*," Kramer discusses some of the formal principles in the novel that reflect Hardy's "lifelong interest in the duality of the apparent and the real."]

The formal principles of the novels before *Tess of the d'Urbervilles* can be thought of as at once proportional and spatial; that is, they help to determine emphases within the material as the plot progresses, and they imply that significance is at least partially external to the individual. Most clearly in *Far from the Madding Crowd* and *The Return of the Native*, those principles literally define the balance and stress of passages of character delineation and such matters as the symbolic value of geographic placement on the verge or in the center of Egdon Heath. The cyclic pattern underlying *The Mayor of Casterbridge* encompasses the progression of the plot as well as the spatial and temporal conditions of the tragic situation, and although in a considerably more abstract manner, so does the idea of universal tragic stature in *The Woodlanders,* as characters alternate in assuming and abandoning the center of attention.

In his last two great novels, which have been most keenly etched in readers' memories as uniquely Hardyan stories (though not all readers admire them equally), the primary formal principles are neither spatial nor proportional. The stories do have spatial schemes, based essentially on the reenactment of similar experiences, which take place in localities of special interrelationships. But in the uniqueness of the novels those spatial schemes are more or less incidental, caused primarily by the necessity for plot and for movement among the characters.

The important formal principles of the late novels are concepts of consciousness—concepts of the manner in which perception of experience shapes the meaning of the experience and, indeed, even constitutes its significance. These principles reflect the Manichean bias of Hardy's philosophical metaphors and his lifelong interest in the duality of the apparent and the real. They are also the natural development from the principles we have examined in the previous novels. The development can perhaps be most readily traced from *The Mayor of Casterbridge* and *The Woodlanders* to *Tess of the d'Urbervilles*—from a position of externality providing significance for the individual (Henchard) to a position of rich but ambiguous individuality-dissolving experience (*The Woodlanders*) to a position in which significance is caused solely by the internal qualities of the subject (Tess). The development continues to *Jude the Obscure,* which offers another consciousness—one not directly involved in the action, that of the narrator—interleaving in a highly complex manner interpretations of reality with those of the protagonist. The abstract formal principles are of course not entirely without previous manifestations in Hardy's work. In *Far from the Madding Crowd* he defines as of the utmost importance in tragic effect the ability of the character for sustained and intense suffering; and in most of his novels the narrator expresses opinions. But it was only after *The Woodlanders* that the abstractions took precedence over concepts of form that include spatial organization. Moreover, his final vision of significance has few points of contact with the prescriptions and restrictions of classical tragic theory. He did not explicitly reject classical theories or examples after *The Woodlanders*—he used the idea of the family curse in both *Tess of the d'Urbervilles* and *Jude the Obscure*—but his sense of the tragic was not confined to characters or dilemmas of classical "correct" dimensions.

Tess of the d'Urbervilles stresses the subjectivity of experience and judgment. In basing the aesthetic effect of his work upon the principle of subjectivity, Hardy broadened a trail rather than blazed one, although I know of no earlier fictional tragedy to employ the concept. The aesthetic energy in subjectiveness was bizarrely thrust upon Western consciousness by Rousseau, especially in his *Confessions,* and its fecundity is still evident. Keats's odes and Wordsworth's *The Prelude,* and such later works as Conrad's and Faulkner's novels, are well known examples of the capacity of the mind to make its own self-significating world. Hardy shares an essentially romantic perception with these writers, but less sophisticated. Although an awareness of the principle is clear in all of his work—I have already remarked upon its appearance in *The Return of the Native*—the full exploitation of subjectivity as an index to tragedy appears first in *Tess of the d'Urbervilles*. It is perhaps partly because tragedy was not an active form during the era of the aggrandizement of common humanity by romanticism (though it does appear in the subgenre of Gothicism in both fiction and drama) that Hardy was the first to structure a tragedy upon the individual's comprehension of himself rather than upon his relation to a social world. ⟨...⟩

Each of Hardy's tragedies is in its own way a brief for the desirability of individual freedom, but in *Tess of the d'Urbervilles* he expands freedom of conscience to include freedom of consciousness, a near anarchy of perception. "The world is only a psychological phenomenon," says Hardy-as-narrator early in the novel (p. 108); and he demonstrates in a variety of ways within the novel the impossibility of objective and detached observation and evaluation of life. The meaning of an action depends not only upon the situation, which in itself is probably unique, but also upon the beholders, who while broadly consistent in their characterizations are not constant.

(Angel's declaration to Tess, following her story of her past, that she is not the woman he married earlier in the day; Tess's later decision that after marrying Angel she was a different person from the one she had been with Alec—these declarations reflect the evanescence of life as surely as they do Tess's and Angel's confusion about morality and their own evolving personalities.)

The emphasis upon subjectivity of experience locates the source of the tragic emotion in *Tess of the d'Urbervilles* within the human consciousness rather than within some sort of relationship between the individual and environment, or between individuals, or between an individual and the moral order of his world. Obviously, there are social and interpersonal relationships, and Hardy does not fail to show how they impinge upon and affect the consciousness of the separate individual. But the tragic emotion itself is subjective, centering in characters essentially isolated within selves that do not remain stable entities even within themselves.

> —Dale Kramer, *Thomas Hardy: The Forms of Tragedy* (Detroit: Wayne State University Press, 1975): pp. 111–14.

RONALD D. MORRISON ON READING AND RESTORATION

[Ronald D. Morrison is the author of "Remembering and Recovering Goblin Market in Rosario Ferre's 'Pico Rico, Mandorico'" and "Humanity Towards Man, Woman and the Lower Animals: Thomas Hardy's Jude the Obscure and the Victorian Humane Movement." In the excerpt below from his article, "Reading and Restoration in *Tess of the d'Urbervilles*," Morrison renders a psychoanalytical reading of the recuperative process.]

In 1894, only three years after Hardy published the volume edition of *Tess of the d'Urbervilles*, Lionel Johnson enunciated what critics have often designated as the novel's biggest flaw. Johnson wrote that he could not rank *Tess* "so high, as certain other of Mr. Hardy's books" because he recognized in it too much "insinuated argument" (236). Further, he noted a "refusal to let the facts of the story convey their own moral, without the help of epigrammatic hints" (236). Johnson's comments represent the beginning of a long-running debate on the narrator of *Tess*. What Johnson called "insinuated argument" other critics have termed "authorial intrusion" (and far worse).[1] Not only are the narrator's comments distracting, but, as many critics have pointed out, the narrator's stance is strongly biased in favor of Tess Durbeyfield.[2] Indeed studies of the manuscript reveal that Hardy revised *Tess* almost obsessively and that in these successive revisions he continued to emphasize Tess's purity and Angel's perverse idealism.[3] What might be the causes for Hardy's extreme reactions to this novel and its heroine?

J. T. Laird, in his study of the manuscript of *Tess of the d'Urbervilles*, suggests three possible solutions to the critical problem represented by the narrator's "intrusions." Readers, he argues, may view the narrator's comments (1) as the author's reaction to the "prevailing ethos of the time"; (2) as part of Hardy's narrative method; or (3) as the voice of the narrator rather than the voice of Hardy (191–92). No doubt all three are accurate in part. Clearly Hardy was attacking one version of the "prevailing ethos" of his time with his thoroughly unsympathetic portrait of Angel Clare. In addition, Hardy chaffed against another result of the "prevailing ethos" when the editors of the *Graphic* forced him to make numerous revisions, which he later resentfully described as the novel's "dismemberment."[4] ⟨. . .⟩ In *Tess,* as in the earlier novels, Hardy's narrator presents a number of distorted views of one woman, Tess Durbeyfield. The narrator, in effect, presents Tess Durbeyfield as a mysterious text that he alone can decipher. Just as the various men in the novel find Tess a puzzling text and constantly strive to interpret her, the narrator presents, in effect, a "reading" or an interpretation of Tess.[6] Just as Hardy later sought to "restore" the printed novel, so the narrator actively works to restore Tess's "wounded name."

The restoration process begins with Hardy's epigraph, which comes from Shakespeare's *Two Gentlemen of Verona:* ". . . Poor wounded name! My bosom as a bed / Shall lodge thee" (I.ii.115–16). This passage, in the context of the play, refers directly to restoring a damaged text. Julia has just received a love letter from Proteus. While her servant Lucetta is in the room, Julia pretends to despise Proteus, tearing the letter into pieces. ⟨. . .⟩

This epigraph suggests a number of parallels between Hardy's novel and Shakespeare's play. Most obviously, both works concern a lover's betrayal, though Julia is eventually reunited with her aptly-named lover. Furthermore, in both works lovers find magic in their lover's name; the name of the beloved becomes a type of fetish, an odd empowerment of language that perhaps makes the name of the beloved more real than the lover. By giving Tess names, the men in the novel (the narrator included) attempt to make or create Tess.[7] Put another way, they attempt to write Tess (or in Hardy's case, to write *Tess*). The narrator, in fact, presents Tess's life as a series of scraps, which he calls "phases." Importantly, several of these phases label Tess; she is both maiden and maiden-no-more and later a woman. Over the course of the novel (and, perhaps it is fair to say, over the course of the novel's publication) Tess receives many other names: wife, deserted wife, adulteress, murderess, and so forth. And Tess receives several surnames; she is both a Durbeyfield and a d'Urberville, and later she is Mrs. Clare, though she dares not go by that name. Already there is a central problem: If the narrator is going to protect Tess's name, which one will he protect? Which name, which quality will he restore?

A partial answer is found in the various prefatory materials to the novel, which also concern reading and restoring texts. The Explanatory Note to the First Edition explains that the chapters "more especially addressed to adult readers" have been restored to the text (27).[8] In his Preface to the Fifth Edition, Hardy voices his thanks to reviewers who "welcomed the tale": "Their words show that they, like the others, have only too largely repaired my defects of narration by their own imaginative intuition" (29). These readers have rescued Tess, restored her, salvaged the dignity that his artistic failings mar. These readers have, in effect, completed the job of the narrator. Indeed I believe that strategy—forcing the reader to complete the narration and thus complete the woman—to be one of Hardy's major objectives in writing *Tess*.

Notes

1. In one notable example, Dorothy Van Ghent calls the narrator's commentary "bits of philosophic adhesive tape" (196).

2. This tendency is not entirely consistent, however. See, for example, Paris (59) and Schweik (17–18). Also see Claridge, who argues *Tess* "is too often caught in the middle of Hardy's own evolving ideas" (332). For a counterview, see Freeman, who argues that Hardy's "watching presence . . . is the most fundamental stability in the novel" (317).

3. Laird's *The Shaping of Tess of the d'Urbervilles* is the most complete study of the manuscript. Mary Jacobus's essay "Tess's Purity" is also useful, especially for exploring how Hardy's revisions altered the presentation of Tess. For example, in the Ur-novel, the Tess character is less admirable and far more straightforward in her relationship with Alec. In the earlier version, Angel, as Jacobus writes, is "scrupulous rather than obsessional" (331) and is much more sympathetic to Tess's plight than in the later version.

4. See Purdy for a concise description of Hardy's revisions of the novel for serial publication (68–70). As Purdy notes, the editors of the *Graphic* deemed several chapters unacceptable, so Hardy published them as separate pieces: "Chaps. 10 and 11, the seduction of Tess by Alec d'Urberville, were printed under the title 'Saturday Night in Arcady' in a Special Literary Supplement of the *National Observer* (Edinburgh), 14 November 1891; Chap. 14, the baptism and death of Tess's baby, was printed under the title 'The Midnight Baptism, A Study in Christianity' in the *Fortnightly Review*, May 1891 . . ." (69). Even though the *Graphic* contains one of the classic instances of Victorian bowdlerization—Angel carting the three milkmaids across the pool in his handy wheelbarrow—Laird remarks that "the First Edition is sometimes less frank than the *Graphic* in describing the feelings and behaviour of Tess and Angel during the courtship period at Talbothays" (158).

6. Though it is not the focus of his chapter on *Tess*, Miller briefly notes the novel's preoccupation with reading and writing (120–26). Also see Michie (112–13) and Thompson.

7. I believe, as Kramer does, that "[a]t times it is difficult to separate the position of the omniscient storyteller (or *persona*) from that of one of the characters" (132). See Lucas on Tess's struggle to break free of these various interpretations (178–79).

8. See note 4 above. All quotations from the novel are taken from the paperback version of the New Wessex Edition.

—Ronald D. Morrison, "Reading and Restoration in *Tess of the d'Urbervilles*," *Victorian Newsletter* no. 82 (Fall 1992): pp. 27–29.

LISA STERNLIEB ON THE OLD TESTAMENT AND TESS' CHARACTER

[Lisa Sternlieb is the author of "*Jane Eyre:* 'Hazarding Confidences'" (1999) and "Molly Bloom: Acting Natural" (1998). In the excerpt below from her article, "'Three Leahs to Get One Rachel': Redundant Women in *Tess of the d'Urbervilles*," Sternlieb discusses the competing myths of the Rachel and Leah story in Genesis with that of Darwin's theory of sexual selection.]

After carrying three other dairymaids across a flooded lane, Angel Clare finally gets his chance with Tess Durbeyfield. "Three Leahs to get one Rachel," he whispers. This essay argues that the unwanted dairymaids, the duped husband on his honeymoon, and the younger sister who replaces the elder find their origins in the story of Jacob and his wives. This biblical tale of sexual selection works in dialogue with Darwin's theory in Hardy's novel. The essay seeks to show that Hardy's concern is not only for the beautiful and beloved Tess, but for Marian, Izz, and Retty, redundant women who would have fared better in biblical times than in late Victorian England. One of the last great Victorian novels destroys the nineteenth-century marriage plot by exposing it as a statistical lie.

Walking to church one Sunday, Tess Durbeyfield and her three fellow dairymaids come across a flooded lane. The young women are rescued by the man each adores, Angel Clare, who carries first Marian, then Izz, then Retty across the pool. When a shy Tess protests that she can climb along the bank without being carried, Angel quickly grabs her. "Three Leahs to get one Rachel," he whispers. This has been a strangely forgotten line in a memorable scene. While much has been made of Hardy's constant comparisons between Tess and Eve, I have found no critics referring to this other crucial story from Genesis. Yet in Angel's off-hand remark Hardy suggests a key to understanding how *Tess of the d'Urbervilles*'s interests in ancient origins, sexual selection, naïve husbands, unmarriageable women and conveniently replaceable sisters converge.

For many years discussions of sexuality in *Tess* focused on the heroine's purity, on Hardy's critique of the double standard and "the social emphasis on virginity." This criticism concentrated on male hypocrisy and men's objectification and victimization of Tess. More recently criticism has implicated Hardy himself in his portrait of Tess. Feminist psychoanalytic critics have shown how Hardy turns Tess into a spectacle, how he betrays his own fascination with her as a sexual being by making her sexuality available to the assumed male reader. What unites this criticism is its emphasis on the male spectator and the male seducer, on masculine prerogative in the mating game. An examination of the Rachel and Leah story, however, shows how Tess is equally invested in a feminine perspective and in a consideration of women's sexual prerogative.

⟨. . .⟩ He chooses this competing myth of origin that comfortingly refutes Darwin's theory of sexual selection while simultaneously affirming the unfortunate evolution of the human species.

In Genesis (29) Jacob journeys from his home to Paddan-aram where he meets and falls in love with Rachel. After laboring for her father, Laban, for seven years, he is allowed to marry her. Jacob wakes the morning after his wedding to find that his father-in-law and veiled bride have duped him, that he has married Rachel's older sister, Leah. Only now that he has consummated his marriage to Leah and promised to labor another seven years for Laban is he allowed to marry Rachel as well. Angel is clearly referring to Jacob's fourteen years of labor. (In a clever but insulting pun Angel associates the three dairymaids with the name Leah [meaning "cow"] while naming his bashful beloved Rachel [meaning "ewe"].) But his words come back to haunt him on his wedding night when he too finds that he has married the "wrong" woman: "You were one person: now you are another," he tells Tess. "The woman I have been loving is not you. . . . [but] another woman in your shape" (179).

Biblical scholars have generally agreed about the meaning of the story of Laban and Leah's deception. Jacob, the younger son who successfully deceives his blind father through the sense of touch, gets his comeuppance in the darkness when his sense of touch deceives him as well.

> The Midrash Bereishit Rabba vividly represents the correspondence between the sin Jacob perpetrates against Isaac and Esau and the wrong Leah and Laban do to Jacob: "And all that night he cried out to her, 'Rachel!' and she answered him. In the morning, 'and, look, she was Leah.' He said to her, 'Why did you deceive me, daughter of a deceiver? Didn't I call out Rachel in the night, and you answered me!' She said, 'There is never a bad barber who doesn't have disciples. Isn't this how your father cried out Esau, and you answered him?'

Hardy takes pains to show that Angel's own dishonesty prior to his marriage results in the bad timing of his confession: "I was going to tell you [about my sexual relationship] a month ago . . . I thought it might frighten you away from me . . . then I thought I would tell you yesterday, to give you a chance at least of escaping me. But I did not.

And I did not this morning, when you proposed our confessing our faults on the landing—the sinner that I was!" (176)

From its beginning the story of Jacob and Rachel is highly unusual, for when Jacob first meets Rachel he immediately kisses her and within several lines declares his love for her. The Bible never tells us that Adam loves Eve or that Abraham loves Sarah, yet Jacob loves Rachel. And this kiss has troubled biblical scholars for centuries, for while brothers kiss brothers, parents kiss children, God kisses Moses at his death, and even heaven and earth kiss, men and women in the Bible do not kiss (Dresner 32). Thus, Hardy alludes to a particularly suggestive biblical account of a man who deeply loves a beautiful woman, yet who willingly agrees to father children with three other women as well.

"The covenant God made with Abraham promised blessing to all humanity through the people that would come from Abraham and Sarah," the biblical scholar Samuel Dresner writes. "So fragile was the chain of the covenant in those early years that it might have broken" had women been forced to remain childless (46). So after Leah gives Jacob four sons and Rachel remains barren, the younger sister gives Jacob her maid Bilhah to mate with. Bilhah gives Jacob another two sons. When Leah thinks her childbearing days are over, she gives Jacob her maid, Zilpah. By Zilpah Jacob has another two sons. Despite the competition between the sisters, Rachel willingly gives her husband back to Leah in exchange for Leah's son Reuben's mandrakes or love apples. Leah bears Jacob two more sons and a daughter. Finally, after watching her husband father eleven children by other women, Rachel is "remembered" by God and she bears him two sons before dying. What are we to make of this strange domestic arrangement? ⟨. . .⟩

⟨. . .⟩ Although Rachel has Jacob's love, the first words she speaks emphasize her desperation and envy, his response to her his own ineffectuality as a husband: "'Give me sons, for if you don't, I'm a dead woman!' And Jacob was incensed with Rachel, and he said, 'Am I instead of God, Who has denied you fruit of the womb?'" (30:1–2).

—Lisa Sternlieb, "'Three Leahs to Get One Rachel': Redundant Women in *Tess of the d'Urbervilles*," *Dickens Studies Annual* 29 (2000): pp. 351–54.

Plot Summary of
Jude the Obscure

Published in 1895 in volume form, *Jude the Obscure* was originally serialized and bowdlerized in *Harper's New Monthly Magazine*, December 1894–November 1895. In this form, the novel's title was first *The Simpletons,* then *Hearts Insurgent.* Hardy's last published full-length novel, with its recurring theme of unmarried people living together or a married couple living separately within the same house, provoked a storm of criticism for its "anti-marriage" doctrines. *The Paul Mall Gazette* retitled the novel Jude the Obscene, the Anglican *Guardian* called it "a shameful nightmare," and the American *World* entitled its review "Hardy the Degenerate." Indeed, the outcry was so intense that Hardy gave up novel writing for good.

Part First is set in Marygreen, a place "as old-fashioned as it was small," it is a community which is based on the village of Fawley in Berkshire, where Hardy's paternal grandmother, Mary Head, had been raised, and which Hardy visited in October 1892. Nevertheless, modernity had made its mark, where "the well-shaft was probably the only relic of the local history that remained absolutely unchanged." In **Chapters 1 and 2**, we are introduced to Mr. Phillotson, the schoolmaster, and Jude Fawley, his former student and admirer—at this time a boy of eleven. Mr. Phillotson, who is leaving for Christminster to take a university degree and expects to be ordained, gives young Jude a book as a farewell present. Jude, at this time, is employed by Farmer Troutham, for the purpose of chasing away rooks from the cornfields by using a noisemaker. However, Jude's sympathy is with the birds, so much so that he forgoes his charge as noisemaker and, instead, feeds the hungry rooks. "A magic thread of fellow-feeling united his own life with theirs. Puny and sorry as those lives were, they much resembled his own." After losing his job, Jude sets out to see Christminster for himself. **Chapters 3 and 4** continue with Jude's quest. Though his ability to see the city from his vantage point outside town is at first obstructed, Jude comes to this spot often and meets a wagon driver who is familiar with Christminster. The wagon driver describes the beauty of that city. "As for music, there's beautiful music everywhere in Christminster."

While walking home one evening, Jude meets up with a quack doctor, Physician Vilbert, an itinerant whose "field [is] more obscure than those of the quacks with capital and an organized system of advertising," and with whom he strikes a bargain. Jude offers to advertise Dr. Vilbert's "celebrated" pills amongst the college men, in exchange for the doctor's procurement of Latin and Greek grammar books. Nevertheless, though Jude has lived up to his end of the contract, the doctor has not. Jude soon finds another way to get the books, however, by including a note to Phillotson when the former schoolmaster sends for his old piano. However, when the long-desired books finally arrive, Jude is quite perturbed to learn that there is no easy word for word method of translating English into either Greek or Latin. The sixteen year-old Jude tries to read Latin and Greek by using a dictionary while, simultaneously, driving the bakery wagon for his aunt's burgeoning business. One evening, Jude stops by the side of a road in order to read aloud a poem by Horace about the setting sun and rising moon, Phoebus and Diana from the *Carmen Saeculare,* an act which causes him to turn his attention to spiritual works. He also decides that, in pursuit of his intended religious studies at Christminster, he must find a way to support himself and, thus, he becomes an ecclesiastical stoneworker. By the age of nineteen, Jude is now gainfully employed in his new trade and lives in town during the week, returning home on Saturday evenings.

A little further on, we learn of Jude's meeting and courtship of the attractive Arabella Donn "a complete and substantial female animal —no more, no less" and her eventual seduction and manipulation of him. One evening, while walking home, Jude becomes preoccupied with a list of his scholarly achievements and dreams of getting his D.D. His daydreaming, however, is interrupted by Arabella Donn who he meets on the way. On the following Sunday, Jude and Arabella stop for tea, sitting in a room with a portrait of Samson and Delilah, a detail which alludes to the biblical story and which is meant to underscore the danger of the relationship on which Jude is about to embark. Indeed, shortly after their first day together, Arabella takes the advice of her two girlfriends to get pregnant as the means for ensuring her marriage to Jude. After several unsuccessful attempts to become intimate with her young suitor, Arabella finally manages to be alone with him. She finally seduces him by repeatedly removing and replacing a cochin's (hen's) egg which she says she carries in her bosom until it hatches. "Then there was little struggle,

Jude making a plunge for it and capturing it triumphantly. Her face flushed; and becoming suddenly conscious he flushed also." Two months later, Arabella tells Jude she is pregnant and the two marry, which causes him to forfeit his plans for Christminster. However, her deceitful personality is soon revealed as Jude becomes aware of a series of lies she has told him, including the feigned pregnancy. Jude realizes by now that they are incompatible. We are reminded of his great-aunt's pronouncement that Jude should never marry as the Fawley family has historically proven themselves to be unlucky in their matrimonial choices. Arabella leaves Jude to join her family in Australia and Jude resolves to go to Christminster once his apprenticeship is over.

Part Second begins three years hence, with Jude finally on his way to Christminster. He is also, at this time, curious about his cousin Sue Bridehead, of whom his grand-aunt said was "of the inimical branch of the family." Jude arrives at Christminster and finds cheap lodgings in a suburb named Beersheba. As he wanders amongst the ancient colleges, he hears the voices of famous men associated with this institution, "the worthies who had spent their youth within these reverend walls." Jude takes a job as a stonemason, and observes that the workmen are merely copying and patching. Nevertheless, Jude accepts employment there while studying late into the night. Shortly thereafter, Jude observes Sue Bridehead working in an ecclesiastical warehouse, a shop containing "little plaster angels on brackets, Gothic-framed pictures of saints, ebony crosses that were almost crucifixes, prayer-books that were almost missals." However, he decides not to speak to her directly as he is still married and is still haunted by his family's propensity for making bad marital choices, "where marriage usually meant a tragic sadness." As it turns out, Sue has brought home statues of Venus and Apollo, which she must conceal from her pious landlady while Jude, in another part of the city, is studying the Greek Testament. "[S]he entered with her heathen load into the most Christian city in the country by an obscure street running parallel to the main one." But all his theological pursuits notwithstanding, Jude is praying to be delivered from temptation. Finally, Jude and Sue meet and decide to pay a visit to Phillotson, but his former schoolmaster does not at first recognize him. Neither has Phillotson pursued his dream, except for possibly becoming a licentiate. As the two walk back from their visit, Sue tells Jude that she must leave Christminster because her landlady took great exception to the pagan statues she brought home. But Jude persuades Sue to stay and take Phillotson up on his offer to give her a teaching job.

Jude's aunt warns him that the townsfolk consider Sue to be unconventional, "a pert little thing" who once walked into a pond "with her petticoats pulled above her knees." At this time, Jude also finds himself evaluating his chances for getting accepted into Christminster and the illusions he has been harboring of the ancient university. "He saw what a curious and cunning glamour the neighborhood of the place had exercised over him." He proceeds to visit a local inn and, upon his return home, finds a rejection letter waiting for him. In response, Jude angrily scrawls a quotation from Job xii.3 on the wall: "*I have understanding as well as you; I am not inferior to you; yea, who knoweth not such things as these.*" Jude becomes completely despondent about his academic and romantic aspirations, and spends the day drinking at a local tavern, criticizing university life with the other patrons. Nevertheless, he is lonesome for Sue and sets out to find her. After spending the night at her house, he finds himself ashamed to look Sue Bridehead in the eye the following morning.

Part Third. Upon hearing that Sue is going to a training college in Melchester, Jude decides to visit her—on a mission to discover the true nature of her relationship to Phillotson as well as disclosing the fact that he is married to Arabella. He soon learns from Sue that she has promised to marry Phillotson at the end of her two-year training. Despite this, Jude remains steadfast in his determination to keep seeing her. Accordingly, Jude finds work and lodgings in Melchester. One afternoon, Jude and Sue go off to visit Wardour Castle (built in 1770–76) and, not surprisingly, Jude is drawn to the religious pictures, "stopping by preference in front of the devotional pictures by Del Sarto, Guido Reni, Spagnoletto, Sassoferrato, Carlor Dolci, and others," while his companion is not. At one point, they realize it is too late to get back, they remain with a shepherd overnight. As it turns out, there is a lot of gossip about Sue having overstayed her leave from school, and Jude's motives become suspect, especially as doubt arises whether he is really her cousin. Shortly thereafter, having been expelled from college, Sue arrives at Jude's lodgings, soaked by a driving rain, in order to ask for his help. While there, she and Jude engage in a long conversation in which the very unconventional Sue Brideshead describes what she has read and why. "'My life has been entirely shaped by what people call a peculiarity in me. I have no fear of men, as such, nor of their books." Sue discloses that she had a "friendly intimacy" with a Christminster undergraduate, a young man with whom she lived, though she refused to yield to his sexual advances. For his part, Jude says his evening prayers, though Sue refuses to. Nevertheless, when they part the next morning, Sue knows intuitively that Jude loves her, but has not yet learned that he is married to Arabella. Meanwhile, the scene shifts to Phillotson in his new position at Shaston. He is planning to save money for his and Sue's anticipated marriage, but soon discovers that Sue has been expelled and that Jude has true feelings for her. Sue soon hears from Jude that he is in fact married, a discovery that leaves her angry at his selfish motivation. Determined now to marry Phillotson, Sue comes to stay with Jude and celebrates a wedding meal there following a church ceremony in which she is married to Phillotson. After Sue leaves, Jude becomes depressed and leaves to attend to his sick aunt. He also writes to Sue, asking that she meet him on his way back from Christminster. While on his way, Jude stops at a tavern for a drink and encounters Arabella, now working there as a barmaid, and agrees to meet her in order to decide what to do with their relationship, while at the same time forgetting his original plan to join Sue. Back in Christminster the next day, Arabella tells Jude she is remarried to someone in Australia. Jude angrily leaves Arabella and soon encounters Sue. Sue and Jude return to Marygreen together where he hopes to get Sue to admit that her marriage to Phillotson is a mistake. Sue, however, will not comment. Part Third concludes with Arabella's letter to Jude that her second husband is joining her in London.

Part Fourth begins with Jude's visit to Sue at Shaston. While waiting for her, he plays his favorite hymn, which moves her, albeit for reasons different from Jude's suggestion that they are alike "at heart." An argument then ensues as to whether they can be friends. Jude accuses Sue of being a flirt, while Sue responds that he is "Joseph the dreamer of dreams. . . . [a]nd a tragic Don Quixote. . . . [a]nd sometimes you are St. Stephen, who, while they were stoning him, could see heaven opened." Jude soon leaves her house. However, when Jude's aunt dies, he contacts Sue asking her to attend the funeral, and she does. Afterwards, Sue brings up the subject of unhappy marriages. She finally does admit her unhappy union with Phillotson, stating that she is anguished by having to acquiesce to his wishes. When Sue and Jude part, they kiss passionately, which causes Jude to believe that he is now alienated from the ministry for the second time, the first diversion being Arabella. Jude proceeds to burn all of his theology books, an act he deems necessary in order to be true to himself. Meanwhile, Sue has returned to her husband, Phillotson, but cannot admit her true romantic passion for Jude, instead describing her feelings as platonic. Nevertheless, it soon becomes apparent to her husband that Sue loves Jude. Phillotson decides to set her free of the marriage. Jude next meets Sue at Melchester, informing her that Arabella has asked him for a divorce. Indeed, Jude considers himself free, so much so that he has reserved a hotel room for them, though Sue protests that she cannot yet be intimate with him. "'But partly, perhaps, because it is by his generosity that I am now free, I would rather not be other than a little rigid.'" Ironically, because the original accommodations are no longer suitable, Jude brings Sue to the inn where he recently spent the night with Arabella. Despite some initial anger and confusion on Sue's part, she is eventually consoled by the fact that Jude did not know of Arabella's second marriage. Sue asks him to recite some lines from Shelley's "Epipsychidion," a poem which champions free love but, alas, he cannot. At the end of Part Fourth, Phillotson tells the school authorities that Sue is missing and they promptly dismiss him. Phillotson receives little support from the townspeople, though a struggle ensues, disrupting the meeting. In the end, Phillotson decides to divorce Sue.

Part Fifth begins a year later, at Aldbrickham, with Sue preferring to live with Jude as lovers so as to avoid the oppressive institution of marriage. "'I think I should begin to be afraid of you, Jude, the moment you had contracted to cherish me under a Government stamp, and I was licensed to be loved on the premises by you.'" It is also true that Sue wants to be in control of their relationship, a control to which Jude acquiesces. And, as further proof of his passivity, it is interesting to note that Jude is now engaged in the business of headstones, a "lower class of handicraft" than his previous cathedral work. A little further on, Arabella visits Jude and Sue and it is then known that Arabella has not in fact remarried. Sue becomes threatened by this news of Arabella's "freedom" and her own unwillingness to marry Jude. Despite all her previous protestations, Sue now agrees to marry him. When Sue decides to visit Arabella the next day, it is clear to the latter that Sue has a claim to Jude. In yet another series of ironic reversals of circumstance, Arabella receives a letter from her Australian husband who, in turn, has felt threatened by Arabella's renewed contact with Jude. Furthermore, Jude agrees to look after Arabella's child, of whom he may or may not be the actual father, and whom Sue allows to call her mother. The day after the boy arrives, it is learned that he is called Father Time, because he looks so old. "He was Age masquerading as Juvenility, and doing it so badly that his real self showed through crevices. . . . [H]is face took a back view over some great Atlantic of Time, and appeared not to care what it saw." Sue and Jude give notice of their wedding and invite Mrs. Edlin, the widow who had previously cared for Jude's deceased aunt. Mrs. Eldin proceeds to tell a lurid tale of a man hanged near the Brown House, a man who may be an ancestor to Sue and Jude. In effect, Mrs. Eldin has given their imminent marriage a sinister setting with the result that Sue and Jude decide not to marry after all. The next scene is situated at the Great Wessex Agricultural show in which we learn Arabella's perceptions of Sue and Jude. "'I am inclined to think that she don't care for him much.'" It is also here that Hardy's symbolic intention in the character of Little Father Time is manifested. When Sue and Jude observe that the child is not having a good time, Little Father Time responds with incredible perception and awareness. He does not like the flowers because he knows they will soon die. Two and a half years pass with Jude and Sue living at Kennetbridge and Jude refusing to work on churches. Indeed, he now bakes cakes at home, and those cakes are in the shapes of buildings, "Christminster cakes," "[a]rcades, gables, east windows and all," thereby signaling his longing for that city. Arabella arrives on the scene during the spring fair. As she explains to Sue, she has now found religion and has come with her friend Anny to attend the dedication of a new chapel. On her way home, Arabella meets Phillotson and lectures him on how he should treat a wife. "'There's nothing like bondage and a stone-deaf taskmaster for taming us women.'" For her part, when Sue returns home, having sold all of Jude's cakes, Jude tells her he wants to return to Christminster and they go.

Part Sixth begins with Jude and Sue arriving as planned on Remembrance Day, the anniversary of the founding of the university. However, upon seeing the young men of the college, Jude becomes concerned that this will turn into "Humiliation Day" for him. Jude proceeds to make a speech to a crowd in which he tells of his failed attempt to succeed, concluding with the observation that something is wrong with society. "'I perceive there is something wrong somewhere in our social formulas.'" When the couple later seek lodgings for their family, one landlady shuns them upon discovering that they are not married and tells them they must leave the next day. All the while, Little Father Time has been reflecting on their almost pariah-like status, claiming that he does not understand why children are born into this world. "[A] brooding undemonstrative horror seemed to have seized him." In fact, the child becomes accusatory when Sue tells him she is pregnant. And, the next morning, tragedy strikes as Sue discovers that all three children are dead, the result of another ironic set of circumstances. It seems that upon finding Sue gone, Little Father Time felt unwanted and, as a result, hanged his two siblings and then himself. Following the funeral, Sue stops the gravedigger, asking to see her dead children. The shock of the sight causes her to give birth to a dead baby. While she is recovering, Sue appears very much changed by the experience, declaring that she must reform. In fact, she has been attending church regularly. And, when Arabella arrives to visit Little Father Time's grave, Sue declares that she is not Jude's wife and leaves, only to be found in church. Sue intends to separate from Jude and return to Phillotson. Further on, when Sue arrives at Phillotson's house, she shrinks away from him when he kisses her. While spending the night with Mrs. Edlin, the latter believes Sue to be in love with Jude and informs Phillotson of her observation. Nevertheless they are married the next morning, with Phillotson promising not to infringe on her privacy. "'It is for our good socially to do this, and that's its justification, if it was not my reason.'" In the meantime, Arabella arrives at Jude's domicile in Christminster where she advises him of Sue's marriage. And her former deviousness still remains as she tries yet a new stratagem for trapping Jude into marrying her. One night, while at a local tavern, Arabella encourages Jude to become drunk in order to get him to her father's house with the sole purpose of his prevailing on Jude to marry his daughter. Indeed, Arabella's father goes so far as to tell Jude he promised as much. And so Jude and Arabella are married, but that marriage, quite predictably, proves to be a disaster as they are incompatible. Jude now decides he must find Sue. When he does, it is a passionate meeting between the two in which Sue tells Jude she still loves him and that she has not given herself to

Phillotson. Later that night Jude returns to Christminster, telling Arabella that he now wants to die, while Sue feels guilty about her love for him and decides that her penance must be to sleep with Phillotson. Meanwhile, Jude reflects on his unrealized dreams. "'I was never really stout enough for the stone trade . . . But I felt I could do one thing if I had the opportunity. I could accumulate ideas, and impart them to others. . . . And it is too late, too late for me!'" And when Mrs. Edlin informs him that Sue is now intimate with Phillotson, Jude becomes very disturbed, and "begins to use terribly profane language about social conventions." Physician Vilbert, the quack doctor whom Jude met earlier in the novel is also there at the request of Arabella. Jude's insults send him away, but not before Arabella can give the doctor some of his own "love-philter." Finally, the narrative ends on Remembrance Day with Jude asleep and Arabella anxious to join the festivities. When Jude awakens, he is alone. He remembers the holiday and recites some verses from Job. Meanwhile, Arabella returns home long enough to discover that Jude has died. Two days later, only Arabella and Mrs. Edlin attend his coffin amidst the sounds of celebration in the background. The story ends with Arabella's prediction that Sue will never find peace on earth until she dies. "'She's never found peace since she left his arms and never will again till she's as he is now!'" ❁

List of Characters in
Jude the Obscure

Jude Fawley – The hero of the novel. A young stonemason of ordinary working-class origins. He is idealistic and imaginative, with ambitions of becoming a student at Christminster University.

Sue Bridehead – Jude's cousin, an intelligent, sensitive, refined and rather unconventional young woman with whom Jude is in love. She marries Phillotson, leaves him to live with Jude and later remarries Phillotson.

Richard Phillotson – A kindly schoolmaster with academic ambitions. He keeps Sue as a pupil-teacher under his training and later marries her.

Arabella Donn – A coarse, sensual young woman who works on her father's pig-farm and also as a barmaid. She marries Jude, then divorces him and marries Cartlett.

Little Father Time – Jude and Arabella's son. He is a solemn, rather anxious, pessimistic child with a prematurely aged appearance.

Aunt Drusilla Fawley – Jude's great-aunt with whom he lives in Mary-green as a boy after he is orphaned.

Mrs. Edlin – An elderly, kindly widow who is a companion to Aunt Drusilla.

George Gillingham – A friend of Phillotson's, he is also a schoolmaster. He tries to give Phillotson advice on his domestic difficulties.

Physician Vilbert – A quack doctor who practices in and around Marygreen.

Mr. Donn – Arabella's father.

Anny – A childhood friend of Arabella's. She is as coarse and cunning as Arabella.

Cartlett – Arabella's second husband whom she marries in Australia, although she is still married to Jude at the time. A coarse, red-faced man, he keeps a tavern.

Uncle Joe and Tinker Taylor – Drinking companions of Jude's in Christminster. ❀

Critical Views on
Jude the Obscure

SUZANNE EDWARDS ON THE SELF-CONSCIOUS CHILD

[Suzanne Edwards is the author of "Robert Browning's 'Saul': Pre-Raphaelite Painting in Verse" (1986). In the excerpt below from her article, "A Shadow from the Past: Little Father Time in *Jude the Obscure*," Edwards discusses the narrative function of Hardy's self-conscious child as underscoring Jude's past mistakes.]

Little Father Time, the self-conscious child in Thomas Hardy's *Jude the Obscure* who hangs himself and his younger brother and sister, has provoked considerable critical commentary over the years. He has been variously interpreted as a grotesque monster, a Christ figure, a prophet of Doom, the choric voice of History, and a symbol of the Modern Spirit.[1] He is, to a degree, all of these. But, perhaps more significantly, he is an extension of his father's personality and temperament. In his essential loneliness and isolation, his hyper-sensitivity, his pessimistic outlook, and his suicidal bent, Father Time is clearly Jude Fawley's child. As such, he appropriately functions to advance the plot and to symbolize the significance of the mistakes Jude has made in the past.

The similarity between Jude and Little Father Time is readily apparent. Sue is the first to comment on the likeness just after the boy comes to Aldbrickham to live with his father. Noting the resemblance between parent and child, Sue exclaims to Jude, "I see you in him!"[2] Though Sue sees Arabella in the boy as well, the resemblance between mother and son is only physical whereas the likenesses between father and son are physical, situational, and psychological.

Both Father Time and the young Jude are described by the narrator in similar terms. Jude, as a child, is presented as slender-framed, "puny and sorry" (pp. 13, 16). He is a "thoughtful" boy, one who appears to have "felt the pricks of life somewhat before his time" (p. 11). His son is "a small, pale" child with "large, frightened eyes" (p. 289). Even more somber than his father had been as a boy, Father Time is described as "... Age masquerading as Juvenility" (p. 290).

Neither Jude nor his son enjoys a happy childhood. After his parents die, Jude comes to live with his great-aunt Drusilla, a sharp-tongued, morose old woman who never disguises the fact that she considers supporting the boy an onerous duty. She impresses upon him that it would be better if he too had died: "It would ha' been a blessing if Goddy-mighty had took thee too, wi' thy mother and father, poor useless boy!" (p. 13). But, since God Almighty did not take Jude, Miss Fawley voices the wish that the schoolmaster had done so when he moved away. "[W]hy didstn't go off with that schoolmaster of thine to Christminster or somewhere?" she asks the boy (p. 18). After the departure of Mr. Phillotson, the friendless child is left alone with his books and his idealistic dreams for the future, convinced he will "be a burden to his great-aunt for life" (p. 17).

Father Time's early years are much the same. Abandoned by his mother, he is raised by grandparents who soon tire of being "encumbered" and ship him, alone, from Australia back to Arabella in England. Since he is not yet old enough to work in her husband's tavern, Arabella does not "know what to do with him" and, in turn, "despatches" him to Jude who has previously not even been aware of the child's existence (pp. 287, 290). Even after coming to live with Jude and Sue, who show him tenderness and affection, Father Time persists in considering himself a burden. He cries to Sue, "I oughtn't to have come to 'ee—that's the real truth! I troubled 'em in Australia, and I trouble folk here. I wish I hadn't been born!" (p. 350). Despite Jude's anxious desire that his son never think, "Let the day perish wherein I was born, and the night in which it was said, There is a man child conceived," the thought cannot be cancelled from the child's mind (p. 288).

Pessimistic by nature and by circumstances, Jude also frequently wishes "that he had never been born" (p. 33) and bemoans the meaninglessness of his "undemanded" existence (p. 19). His joy at receiving his first Latin and Greek texts is obliterated by his realization of how difficult it will be to educate himself, and "under the crushing recognition of his gigantic error Jude continued to wish himself out of the world" (p. 33). Throughout his life, Jude has "Modern" feelings of doubt, confusion and pessimism. ⟨. . .⟩

For Jude, the noises and glares do increase as he grows older whereas Little Father Time is born into a recognition of them. The doctor who comes to attend to the three dead children declares that boys like Father Time are "the outcome of new views of life. They seem to see all its terrors before they are old enough to have staying power to resist them" (p. 354). Father Time is presented from the first as "singularly deficient in all the usual hopes of childhood" (p. 303). He never experiences the carefree days associated with youth. Even as a boy he is oppressed by what Wordsworth calls "the inevitable yoke" of the material world. Wordsworth's warning to the young,

> Full soon thy Soul shall have her earthly freight,
> And custom lie upon thee with a weight,
> Heavy as frost, and deep almost as life![3]

has prematurely become reality for Little Father Time. The very things that lift the spirits of others seem to intensify the little boy's dejection. As he journeys by train to his father's home in Aldbrickham, across the aisle from him sits a woman whose playful kitten entertains the passengers, all of them "except the solitary boy bearing the key and ticket, who, regarding the kitten with his saucer eyes, seemed mutely to say: 'All laughing comes from misapprehension. Rightly looked at there is no laughable thing under the sun'" (p. 289). Several years later, every effort of Jude and Sue still proves vain to rouse him from his inherent despondency. At the Wessex Agricultural Show, Father Time cannot enjoy the roses, for as he explains, "I should like the flowers very, very much, if I didn't keep on thinking they'd be all withered in a few days!" (p. 312).

Notes

1. See Walter K. Gordon, "Father Time's Suicide Note in *Jude the Obscure*," *Nineteenth-Century Fiction*, 22 (1967), 298–300; Ian Gregor, *The Great Web: The Form of Hardy's Major Fiction* (London: Faber and Faber, 1974): Ward Hellstrom, "A Study of *Jude the Obscure*," Diss. University of Illinois, 1961; Norman Holland, Jr., "*Jude the Obscure*: Hardy's Symbolic Indictment of Christianity," *Nineteenth-Century Fiction*, 9 (June 1954), 50–60; Lewis B. Horne, "Hardy's Little Father Time," *South Atlantic Quarterly*, 73 (1974), 213–23; and Frederick F. P. MacDowell, "Hardy's 'Seeming or Personal Impressions': The Symbolical Use of Image and Contrast in *Jude the Obscure*," *Modern Fiction Studies*, 6 (Autumn 1960), 233–50.

2. Thomas Hardy, *Jude the Obscure* (New York: Bantam Books, 1981), p. 292. All further references to the novel appear in the text.

3. William Wordsworth, "Ode: Intimations of Immortality from Recollections of Early Childhood" in *Selected Poems and Prefaces*, ed. Jack Stillinger (Boston: Houghton Mifflin Company, 1965), p. 189, ll. 126–28.

    —Suzanne Edwards, "A Shadow from the Past: Little Father Time in *Jude the Obscure*," *Colby Library Quarterly* 23, no. 1 (March 1987): pp. 32–34.

[Regenia Gagnier is the author of "The Law of Progress and the Ironies of Individualism in the Nineteenth Century" (2000) and "Productive, Reproductive and Consuming Bodies in Victorian Aesthetic Models" (2000). In the excerpt below from the article, "Further Reflections on Sympathetic Identification," Gagnier identifies a variety of aesthetic models used by Hardy as a social critique of work, education and marriage.]

⟨. . .⟩ In the remainder of this essay, I shall argue that the history of aesthetics embedded in Thomas Hardy's novel *Jude the Obscure* (1895) provides us with a much richer aesthetic than that represented in current theory, and that this historical aesthetic can tell us much about the social good. For although Rorty construes aesthetics in contrast to reason, the particular history of aesthetics of which Hardy's novel partakes reminds us of when the claims for feeling and imagination had a much broader scope, pertaining to ethics, political economy, and biology. I am especially eager to revive this history just now, when its social utility has been denied and its contested terrains have been reduced to what is now monolithically labeled "*the* Aesthetic." In *Jude,* Hardy employs the ethical, political economic, and biological models of aesthetics current in his time only to show how his characters are systematically denied access to aesthetic experience. In reflecting on this prohibition through the process I have called a sympathetic understanding of difference, a reader can then use reason to begin to construct the kinds of social alternatives Hardy anticipated in his critiques of work, education, and the institution of marriage. ⟨. . .⟩

In *Jude,* the novel as a whole may be seen, H. M. Daleski has argued, as Jude and Sue's attempt to carve out an ethics, an autonomy, of will in the face of necessity. Daleski interprets what might be seen as Sue's cruel virginity as rather an attempt at autonomy or "self-containment." Sue says, regarding her ascesis, that "I never yielded myself to any lover. . . . I have remained as I began," and the constant references to her epicene nature, her "curious unconsciousness of gender," indicate a technology of the self, if a uniquely individualist one, opposed to her social role as a woman. Jude's history as the quintessential autodidact is similar. He studies the Bible and classical languages as if individual talent and merit could surmount social barriers. With their final chastisement, their wills are broken and every attempt at their self-creation has been defeated—Jude's for education and for meaningful labor, Sue's for female independence, their collective dream of unity.

The second aesthetic tradition of the Victorians was the political economic, which focused upon the producer of the work and conditions of production: this was Ruskin's aesthetic, Morris's after him, and, of course, Marx's and generations of Marxists. (In its particularly historical aspect, it was also Hegel's.) At Christminster Jude reads "the numberless architectural pages around him" as Ruskin "reads" (his own term) the cathedrals at San Marcos or Amiens. Jude reads, "naturally, less as an artist-critic of their forms than as an artizan and comrade of the dead handicraftsmen whose muscles had actually executed those forms" (103). Ruskin had written in 1851, "Go forth again to gaze upon the old cathedral front, where you have smiled so often at the fantastic ignorance of the old sculptors: examine once more those ugly goblins and formless monsters, and stern statues, anatomiless and rigid; but do not mock at them, for they are signs of the life and liberty of every workman who struck the stone." Contrary to an aesthetics located in the object (Plato's) or in the perceiver (Kant's or Burke's), the political economists of art (Ruskin's phrase) began with the very body of the artist. ⟨. . .⟩ Written well after the theory had been discredited, much of the outrage in *Jude* is against a society that so undervalues its producers. And Hardy's terms are those of political economy: from the beginning Jude is conscious of himself, of his "unnecessary life" (36), as part of Malthus's "surplus population," and his children die "because we are too menny" (356).

When Little Father Time comes to live with his father, Jude's socialist discursus on parenting hearkens back to Ruskin's *Unto This Last:* "the beggarly question of parentage—what is it, after all? What does it matter . . . whether a child is yours by blood or not? All the little ones of our time are collectively the children of us adults of the time, and entitled to our general care. The excessive regard of parents for their own children, and their dislike of other people's is, like class-feeling, patriotism, save-your-own-soulism, and other virtues, a mean exclusiveness at bottom" (293). ⟨. . .⟩

Physiological aesthetics pervades *Jude the Obscure.* From the beginning, Jude possesses a distinct temperament. Uncommonly sensitive to the sufferings of birds (34), pigs (36), rabbits (234), and women (289), he *expects* others to feel as he does. On being moved by a church hymn, Jude assumes that the composer will sympathize with his own ambition. He is shocked and disappointed to find, upon seeking him out, that the composer has given up music for trade (214–15).

Jude and Sue's heightened "sensitivity" (305) is manifested not only in sympathy towards vulnerability but also in their mutual recoil from vulgarity. Jude, of course, castigates himself for his innate and vicious attraction to women and liking for spirits. Yet he cannot help his aesthetic sense feeling violated when Arabella reveals a hairpiece on their wedding night: he feels a sudden distaste for her, "a feeling of sickness," and fears that she may have "an instinct towards artificiality . . . [may] become adept in counterfeiting" (79). When Arabella sells his photograph before she emigrates, Jude perceives "the utter death of every tender sentiment in his wife" (93). He regrets their marriage, "based upon a temporary feeling which had no necessary connection with affinities that alone render a life-long comradeship tolerable" (90). He shares those affinities with Sue, who is "light and slight, of the type dubbed elegant" (109) and variously described as "uncarnate" (207), a "disembodied phantom hardly flesh at all" (265, 413), and "a phantasmal bodiless creature" (279). The cruelty that Sue's bodilessness entails for her husbands is forgiven by Jude's agonized "all that's best and noblest in me loves you, and your freedom from everything that's gross has elevated me" (285). Sue insists upon this sublimation and continually condemns the carnal Arabella as "low," "coarse," and "vulgar" (285, 287, 290). Indeed, we might understand Arabella as instinctively acting upon Hume's famous dictum that "Reason is and ought only to be the slave of the passions, and can never pretend to any other office than to serve and obey them," in which a minimal reason relates means to ends but makes no claims concerning the rightness of ends. Jude's communal feeling as a stonemason can no more be reconciled with these hierarchical tastes than his feeling for the laborer can be reconciled with his chastisement of the body. One aesthetic is productivist; the other is discriminatory and ascetic.

> —Regenia Gagnier, "Further Reflections on Sympathetic Identification," *Rereading Texts/Rethinking Critical Presuppositions: Essays in Honour of H. M. Daleski,* Shlomith Rimmon-Kenan, Leona Toker and Shuli Barzilai, editors. Frankfurt am Main; Berlin; Bern; New York; Paris; Wien: Peter Lang GmbH (1997): pp. 166–70.

William R. Goetz on the Distinction Between Divorce and Marriage

[William R. Goetz is the author of *Henry James and the Darkest Abyss of Romance* (1986) and "Criticism and Autobiography in James's Prefaces" (1979). In the excerpt below from his article, "The Felicity and Infelicity of Marriage in *Jude the Obscure*," Goetz discusses the problematic distinction between divorce and marriage.]

By calling the marriage laws his "machinery," Hardy suggests, as he did in the letter to Gosse, that the institution of marriage is important to the novel but only as a means, not as an end; the end is "tragedy" itself. The statement does admit, though, that the novel's theme has to do with marriage laws, and specifically that the novel seeks to call into question the institution of marriage on the grounds of natural morality. Hardy's opinion that a marriage based on "cruelty" is "essentially and morally no marriage" implies that the novel refers to two different notions of marriage. Civil marriage sanctioned by society may find itself at variance with a more natural form of marriage, one that does not depend on social conventions to validate it. This implicit distinction between two conceptions of marriage is based on the explicit distinction between "civil law" and the "law of nature." Ideally, the relation between these two laws is not so much one of opposition as of "enunciation," wherein the human code of law articulates or speaks the law of nature, which remains dumb. We must not, however, overlook Hardy's parenthetical comment that this model of enunciation, attributed here to Diderot, is in need of "some qualification"—a qualification that Hardy does not supply but which the novel itself, as I shall argue, will supply for him. The Postscript, in any case, promptly forgets the need for "qualification" and proceeds to an attractively straightforward conclusion concerning the novel's theme. If civil marriage deviates from the law of nature by becoming cruel, it "should be dissolvable," presumably through divorce or annulment. The novel would demonstrate the perversion of a marriage that strays from the laws of nature into cruelty and yet cannot be corrected through divorce. Paradoxically, it would be the very lack of authority, or the groundlessness, of such a marriage that would provide the "foundation" for Hardy's own tragic work. ⟨. . .⟩

Thus the opposition between marriage and divorce, in which divorce is seen as the antidote to a cruel marriage, already breaks down, and the relation between the two states becomes much more problematic. The whole novel, Hardy wrote to Gosse, was to be constructed on "contrasts,"[4] the foremost of which the author defined in his original preface as "a deadly war waged between flesh and spirit" (Norton *Jude,* p. 5). These contrasts, though, as we shall see, are not so much relations of mutual exclusion, when one term is to be preferred to the other, as they are double binds, when the inadequacy of one term gives way only to the inadequacy of the other. Such will be the structure of Hardy's "tragedy." Marriage finds its place in this tragedy not only as a social theme but as an institution whose form lends itself to the shape of the novel Hardy is trying to write. ⟨. . .⟩

Insofar as marriage furnishes the "machinery" for *Jude the Obscure,* the novel becomes an exploration of the marriage contract considered both as "letter" and as speech act. These two aspects of marriage, and especially the latter one, constitute the basis for Hardy's critique of marriage as an institution. Indeed, the unhappiness that all the main characters encounter in their marriages is to some extent analyzed as a consequence of the various "infelicities," in Austin's special sense, to which the act of marriage can succumb. Certain episodes in the novel can practically be read as textbook examples of "infelicity" in performative acts. Such is the mock marriage that Sue and Jude perform just hours before her real wedding to Phillotson (III, 7). Placing her arm in his for the first time, "almost as if she loved him," Sue insists on walking up the church nave to the altar railing and back down, "precisely like a couple just married." The act is infelicitous, of course, because of the absence of both an officiating minister and a marriage oath spoken by the two parties. Jude finds Sue's rash mimicking of the marriage act irresponsible, and says to himself, "She does not realize what marriage means!" Sue's toying with the wedding ceremony is, among other things, an instance of her ability to hurt the feelings of Jude, who finds her behavior here "merciless." Another example of an irresponsible tampering with the convention of marriage is given by Arabella when she consents to marriage with the man in Australia even though she is already married to Jude. This entire subplot, which includes Arabella's divorce from Jude and her remarriage, now within the proper forms, to the man she met in Australia, exemplifies a speech act that "misfires" (a subcategory of "infelicity" for Austin) and is then rectified by a return to the required conventions.

Note
4. Letters, II, 99.

—William R. Goetz, "The Felicity and Infelicity of Marriage in *Jude the Obscure*," *Nineteenth-Century Fiction* 38, no. 2 (September 1983): pp. 190–94.

ELIZABETH LANGLAND ON THE ELUSIVE SUE BRIDEHEAD

[Elizabeth Langland is the author of "Enclosure Acts: Framing Women's Bodies in Braddon's Lady Audley's Secret" (2000) and "Nation and Nationality: Queen Victoria in the Developing Narrative of Englishness" (1997). In the excerpt below from her article, "A Perspective of One's Own: Thomas Hardy and the Elusive Sue Bridehead," Langland discusses Sue Bridehead's narrative function as a mirror to Jude's limited point of view.]

That Sue Bridehead has resisted satisfactory analysis points both to problems in the formal conception of *Jude* and to the inadequacies of its point of view in conveying a growing sensitivity to other versions of the novel's central experiences. An omniscient narrator, such as Hardy offers in *Jude,* should be a guarantee of reliability, but Hardy's final narrator eludes and evades. And, for the first time, Hardy lets the perspective of a single character, Jude Fawley, dominate the story. To complicate matters further, it is not clear to what extent Jude's perspective is judged by the narrator, or even, as criticism has made clear, to what extent Hardy himself is involved in his narrator's and character's perspectives. In light of these complications, inconsistencies in Sue Bridehead's character and behavior call for reassessment.

We must disentangle Sue's character from the problematic narrative point of view which presents her—a point of view primarily Jude's, but buttressed by the narrator's. To do so, we confront questions of character autonomy and the matrix for judging character. As

James saw, we cannot simply wrest character from the context of narrative technique and point of view. In discussing Sue's character, we must continually account for the novel's point of view which is closely allied with Jude's experience and with a man's perspective on an unconventional woman. And, any effort to resolve questions about Sue's personality must take into account the relationships among mimesis, narrative technique, and character development.

In this larger context, we recognize that Jude's primacy in the novel must shape Sue's role in it, much as in *Tess of the D'Urbervilles* the eponymous character determines and limits the representation of Alec D'Urberville and Angel Clare. In *Jude the Obscure*, Arabella and Sue clearly have as one primary function their appeal to opposite poles in the protagonist's nature: the fleshly and the spiritual. Such an observation has become commonplace, but its consequences for character representation have great importance. Hardy's last novel does not imitate Sue and Jude equally. It imitates the way in which one credulous and naive, but well-intentioned, man, Jude, confronts a world which he sees as increasingly inimical to his desires and goals. He is limited by the society in which he finds himself, by what Hardy calls the "hereditary curse of temperament," and by the conventionality of his own nature. Thus, one of Sue Bridehead's other narrative functions is to unmask the deep-seated assumptions which baffle Jude's hopes. That we come to recognize his personal limitations is essential to a tragic denouement which finds him partially responsible for his fate, not merely a pawn in society's or the universe's machinations. His share of responsibility gives Jude a tragic stature.

This imitation, with its focus on Jude's experience and his point of view, accords with the subject Hardy initially anticipated, the story of a young man "'who could not go to Oxford'—His struggles and ultimate failure. Suicide." But, in correspondence with Edmond Gosse after completing the work in 1895, Hardy admits his subject has broadened, stating that his novel is concerned first with the "labours of a poor student to get a University degree, and secondly with the tragic issues of two bad marriages. . . ." The new subject, now added to the original topic, potentially conflicts with full examination of the first, since it calls for examination of the positions and perspectives of both personalities in a marriage. Clearly feeling the increasing interest of his Sue plot, Hardy confessed to Florence Henniker in August 1895, "Curiously enough, I am more interested in the Sue story than in any I have written." Furthermore, dissatisfaction with his representation of Sue kept Hardy tinkering with her character through several revisions of the novel. ⟨...⟩

That Sue is enmeshed in Jude's limited point of view, then, helps account for our sense of inconsistencies in her character. We attempt to judge as a personality in her own right a figure intended to serve merely to define another personality. Often, when Jude looks at his cousin, he in fact gazes into a mirror which reflects the image of his own ambivalence. He finds Sue "almost an ideality" (p. 114), "almost a divinity" (p. 174), "vision" (p. 223), "ethereal" (p. 224), "uncarnate" (p. 224), "disembodied creature" (p. 294), "sweet, tantalizing phantom" (p. 294), but he cannot ask whether this perceived spirituality is a reflection of her essence or an image of his fear that the fleshliness embodied in Arabella will once again ensnare him. It is Jude who tells us Sue is unpredictable and inconsistent: "her actions were always unpredictable" (p. 211), or "Possibly she would go on inflicting such pains again and again ... in all her colossal inconsistency" (p. 210), or he "decided that she was rather unreasonable, not to say capricious" (p. 190), a "riddle" (p. 160), "one lovely conundrum" (p. 162).

His tendency to blame his cousin in this "gentle" way often reveals Jude's rationalizations of his own failures to act decisively as well. Jude has a keen eye for Sue's departures from candor, but he does not question his own consistency or honesty in concealing his marriage to Arabella from Sue. Interpretations of Jude's interview with his cousin, Sue, after she has run away from Melchester Boarding School focus on the radical inconsistency of her behavior, yet that behavior appears in a different light when we remember that Jude, too, is withholding information—his marriage to Arabella—and consequently behaving inconsistently. He cannot respond to Sue in expected ways, failing to kiss her when "by every law of nature and sex a kiss was the only rejoinder that fitted the mood and the moment. ... [But Jude] had, in fact, come in part to tell his own fatal story. It was upon his lips; yet at the hour of this distress he could not disclose it" (p. 189). Jude chides Sue for her frigidity, but never questions the conventional attitudes which underlie his assumption that it is all right to sleep with Arabella despite his relationship with Sue, or that mere sexual intimacy makes Arabella more his wife than Sue with whom he shares intimacies of a more substantial kind.

If we see Sue as merely a narrative device to reveal Jude, we need not trouble ourselves with these "inconsistencies" in her character. But Sue refuses to be read as a device. Although the critical literature acknowledges limitations in Jude's point of view, it rarely accounts for the resultant distortions in its judgment of Sue. Its failure to do so leads to the problematic conclusion that Sue is what Jude, despite his limitations, thinks she is.

—Elizabeth Langland, "A Perspective of One's Own: Thomas Hardy and the Elusive Sue Bridehead," *Studies in the Novel* 12, no. 1 (Spring 1980): pp. 12–15.

Patrick R. O'Malley on the Role of the Supernatural

[Patrick R. O'Malley is the author of "'The Church's Closet': Confessionals, Victorian Catholicism and the Crisis of Identification" (2001) and "J. P. Clark and the Example of Shakespeare" (1978). In the excerpt below from his article, "Oxford's Ghosts: *Jude the Obscure* and the End of the Gothic," O'Malley discusses the role of the supernatural as an expression of the tragic elements within the novel.]

In an 1896 article entitled "Concerning *Jude the Obscure*," Havelock Ellis praised Thomas Hardy's novel for resisting the tendency toward the fantastic medievalism—a sort of neo-Gothicism—that Ellis saw infecting not only Walter Scott's work but much of nineteenth-century fiction: "Those jerry-built, pseudo-mediaeval structures which [Scott] raised so rapidly and so easily, still retain, I hope, some of the fascination which they possessed for us when we were children." ⟨...⟩

What Ellis calls "melodrama" may be located in part in the vague sense of the supernatural that lurks just outside the frame of Hardy's novels. That is, while Hardy's tragedies usually seem to derive from the stubbornnesses and blindnesses of individual nature, that nature itself always hints at the suppressed supernatural forces that take overt form in the Gothic traditions of the nineteenth century.

This may indeed be the descent into vulgar fantasticism that Ellis detected in Hardy's early novels. Yet *Jude* continues to stage its tragedy as the horrible trauma of the past's eruption into the present, an eruption that takes the form of seemingly supernatural terror, the technique of the Gothic novel itself. Significantly, it is precisely the portrayal of this eruption that Ellis finds weakest, that is, most dependent upon the neo-Gothicisms of Scott's influence:

> Only at one point, it seems to me, is there a serious lapse in the art of the book, and that is when the door of the bedroom closet is sprung open on us to reveal the row of childish corpses. Up to that one admires the strength and sobriety of the narrative, its complete reliance on the interests that lie in common humanity. We feel that here are real human beings of the sort we all know, engaged in obscure struggles that are latent in the life we all know. But with the opening of that cupboard we are thrust out of the large field of common life into the small field of the police court or the lunatic asylum, among the things which for most of us are comparatively unreal. (18–19) ⟨. . .⟩

While Ellis's reading positions Hardy's text as the exemplar of a realist modernism, this should not obscure the fact that the geography of *Jude*'s Christminster is the geography of the Gothic, of a medievalizing and decrepit architecture and an equally medievalizing Catholicism:

> Down obscure alleys, apparently never trodden now by the foot of man, and whose very existence seemed to be forgotten, there would jut into the path porticoes, oriels, doorways of enriched and florid middle-age design, their extinct air being accentuated by the rottenness of the stones. It seemed impossible that modern thought could house itself in such decrepit and superseded chambers. (125)

The moldering city is approached first through its Gothic architecture, its oriels and secret pathways eerily reminiscent of the mazes of monasteries and fortresses that confuse and contain Ann Radcliffe's heroines. And it is further significant that Jude the Obscure himself, with his mock-hagiographic epithet, is a stone mason who is attracted not only to "gothic free-stone work" but also to the construction of ecclesiastical carving and the iconography of Romanist and Ritualist Catholicism: "In London he would probably have become specialized and have made himself a 'moulding mason,' a 'foliage sculptor'—perhaps a 'statuary'" (123). Hardy's progression of specialties here moves from the general decorative arts through the imitation of living things to "statuary," itself at the very heart of the nineteenth-century British debate over idolatry, ritual, and history, a debate with its roots in the iconoclastic movements under Henry VIII and ultimately Cromwell.

In fact, composed almost precisely a century after Austen's *Northanger Abbey*, Hardy's *Jude* also attempts to rewrite the conventions of the Gothic for a new century. Like Austen's novel, *Jude* both draws upon and resists its Gothic forebears; but whereas *Northanger Abbey* ultimately rejects the Gothic traditions of sexual and religious deviance as foreign to English national identity, *Jude* makes those characteristics the very fabric of the British cultural inheritance. Instead of condemning the closet with the dead children as a flaw in this novel's construction, as did Havelock Ellis, I read that moment of "unreality" as central to the novel's construction of the path of sexual deviance, here written as the horror of the traditional bind of marriage itself, and religious oppression, here exemplified by Ritualist Anglicanism. This analysis necessarily re-writes Hardy to some extent back into the nineteenth century rather than seeing in him the unambiguous harbinger of modernism. And it suggests that the Gothic had not yet given up its hold on the Victorian novelist of the 1890s, even a novelist so central to our understanding of the proto-modernist canon as Thomas Hardy. *Jude the Obscure,* like the novels of Radcliffe, constructs its fatal chain of events in conjunction with an increasingly tangled discourse of sexual and religious deviance—not Roman Catholicism, but Anglo-Catholicism, which the novel itself presents as a new and oppressive force in England. ⟨. . .⟩

Indeed, the legal bond of marriage is itself consistently represented as a perverse bondage. "For a man and woman to live on intimate terms when one feels as I do is adultery, in any circumstances, however legal," declares Sue to her husband, Richard Phillotson, before their separation (285). If Jude's wife, Arabella, represents a type of monstrous voluptuousness, relying on the conventions of marriage only when they will advance her sexual and economic desires, Phillotson is yet worse, an ecclesiastically-sanctioned rapist as he approaches Sue after her return to him:

> There was something in Phillotson's tone now which
> seemed to show that his three months of remarriage with
> Sue had somehow not been so satisfactory as his magna-
> nimity or amative patience had anticipated. [...] He put
> his arm round her to lift her up. Sue started back.
> "What's the matter?" he asked, speaking for the first
> time sternly.
> "You shrink from me again?—just as formerly!"
> "No, Richard—I—I—was not thinking—[...] It is my
> duty!"
> Placing the candlestick on the chest of drawers he led
> her through the doorway, and lifting her bodily, kissed her.
> A quick look of aversion passed over her face, but
> clenching her teeth she uttered no cry. (478–79)

Like Bram Stoker's Mina, Sue awaits a monstrous version of connu-
bial sex with horror but with no resistance. It is an encounter that
Jude will quickly describe as a type of Radcliffean Gothic novel gone
wrong, a narrative in which the free-thinking woman, having
resisted the advances of the story's villain, does not escape his
clutches but instead gives herself to him:

> [S]he was once a woman whose intellect was to mine like a
> star to a benzoline lamp: who saw all my superstitions as
> cobwebs that she could brush away with a word. Then bitter
> affliction came to us, and her intellect broke, and she veered
> round to darkness. Strange difference of sex, that time and
> circumstance, which enlarge the views of most men, narrow
> the views of women almost invariably. And now the ulti-
> mate horror has come her giving herself like this to what she
> loathes, in her enslavement to forms! (482)

From Sue's embrace of "darkness" to the "ultimate horror" of self-
immersion in a loathed "enslavement," the language of Hardy's text
evoke's Radcliffe's Gothic. But whereas for Radcliffe, the horror lies in
the renunciation of heterosexual courtship and marriage represented
by the convent, Jude locates it in conventional married life itself.

Further, the eruption of the past into the present—little Jude's
killing of Sue's children and his own subsequent suicide—is presented as an image from the Gothic tradition itself:

> A shriek from Sue suddenly caused him to start round. He
> saw that the door of the room, or rather closet—which had

seemed to go heavily upon its hinges as she pushed it back—was open, and that Sue had sunk to the floor just within it. Hastening forward to pick her up he turned his eyes to the little bed spread on the boards; no children were there. He looked in bewilderment round the room. At the back of the door were fixed two hooks for hanging garments, and from these the forms of the two youngest children were suspended, by a piece of box-cord round each of their necks, while from a nail a few yards off the body of little Jude was hanging in a similar manner. (409)

—Patrick R. O'Malley, "Oxford's Ghosts: *Jude the Obscure* and the End of the Gothic," *Modern Fiction Studies* 46, no. 3 (Fall 2000): pp. 646–48, 650–51.

PAUL PICKREL ON THE FALL OF PHAETHON

[Paul Pickrel is the author of "Lionel Trilling and Mansfield Park" (1987) and "*Bleak House:* The Emergence of Theme" (1987). In the excerpt below from his article, "*Jude the Obscure* and the Fall of Phaethon," Pickrel discusses the parallels between Hardy's novel with the myth of Phaethon, a youth of high ambitions which ultimately fail.]

⟨. . .⟩ May identifies the male fantasy with the myth of Phaethon, a youth scoffed at by his friend for claiming to be the son of Phoebus Apollo. When Phaethon complains of the taunt to his mortal mother (the story goes) she sends him off for confirmation from the sun-god himself. At first his father is too brilliant; Phaethon has to hesitate at a distance to get used to the blinding light. But when he finally approaches, his father not only acknowledges paternity at once but in proof swears to grant the boy any one wish he may make. Phaethon of course wants to drive the chariot of the sun across the heavens for a single day. Apollo repents his hasty oath; he knows the task is beyond the youth's strength. But a promise is a promise, as Phaethon is not the last adolescent to point out when he wants to drive the family car just this once; he gets to drive the chariot but with disastrous results. He cannot hold the course; he comes too near the earth and seas dry up, deserts are created, mountains belch fire. Finally Jove himself has to stop the ruinous journey with a thunderbolt, and the adventure ends with Phaethon's long fall from the heavens.

The story recalls the myth of Icarus and other mighty falls. It recalls Erik Erikson's discovery that, while little girls playing with blocks like to create pleasant interior spaces and attractive entrances, little boys like (among other things) to pile up the blocks as high as they will go and then watch them fall down: "the contemplation of ruins is a masculine specialty." The masculine story may have its basis in the anatomy of the male or in his role in reproduction or in other aspects of male sexuality; it has its terrible analogue in the accounts of young men "totalling" automobiles in every evening newspaper. ⟨. . .⟩

Clearly *Jude the Obscure* tells a story of the same general type as the Phaethon myth: a youth of high ambition seeks to follow a noble course and fails. But it is even more to the point that the book is pervaded by the attitudes characteristic of what I have called the Phaethon personality. Some of these attitudes occur in Jude, others in Sue (this may make more sense of Hardy's assertion that they seem like two halves of the same person than anything else does), and some of the attitudes inform the book itself.

A good many of the parallels, though very important and central to the argument, are too obvious to be elaborated. There is, first of all, Jude's "need of achievement," his "restless urge to achieve something outstanding," which is the point of departure for the whole book. Whether this is accompanied by "an unrealistically high evaluation of [his] abilities" it is impossible to say, because the book never provides any practical test of what he can do intellectually; certainly the event proves that he has sadly overestimated his "chances of success." Then there is Jude's isolation from his peers, which seems to be almost complete. We hear of no playmate in childhood; at no time in his life does he have a friend of his own age and sex that the reader hears of. When he accompanies Arabella home after one of their first outings he is embarrassed to find her parents and some of their neighbors in the house; in a particularly inept phrase Hardy says that "they did not belong to his set or circle," but this is the only hint we ever have that Jude could claim membership in any social group, and the rather smart connotations of the word *set* are so absurdly inappropriate for a village loner like Jude that we can only conclude that the sentence is too careless to be taken seriously. Throughout his years of growing up Jude shows the "striking absence of emotional bonds to others" typical of the Phaethon personality; not only does he have no friends but the only relative he knows is the old great-aunt with whom he lives, and she makes no secret that he is a burden to her; she is anything but what is described in contemporary idiom as a warm and nurturing person. Jude's "most important emotional tie" in adolescence is "with an older man," the schoolmaster Phillotson, and that tie exists almost wholly in fantasy, since Phillotson left Marygreen when Jude was a small boy.

One of the less obvious attitudes shared by the novel and the Phaethon personality is the concern with being in control, a concern that mainly manifests itself in the novel in the almost compulsive patterning of characters and events. The main characters, for instance, consist of two pairs, one male, the other female, with each pair carefully balanced against the other and carefully contrasted within itself. Each of the male characters has a wise old counselor who emerges from his past as needed; they are not very surprisingly of different sexes, like the old woman and the old man who bob out of a mechanical clock; the Widow Edlin appears when Jude needs her and Gillingham does the same for Phillotson. Physician Vilbert, the quack doctor who is a survivor of the timeless folk past, an old man at the beginning of the book but young enough to become Arabella's third husband at the end, balances Little Father Time, the prematurely aged prophet of the urban future, who ends a wizened child suicide. The characters move back and forth in obedience to the laws of permutation and combination as predictably as the dancers in a country dance balance to their partners at the caller's command.

Hardy himself was aware of this aspect of the book. He said that "the rectangular lines of the story were not premeditated, but came by chance: except, of course, that the involutions of four lives must necessarily be a sort of quadrille." The logic of this last is not impeccable; four is almost the standard number of central characters in the English novel—writers as dissimilar as Jane Austen, George Eliot, and D. H. Lawrence have started out with two young women and their suitors without necessarily ending up with "a sort of quadrille."

—Paul Pickrel, "*Jude the Obscure* and the Fall of Phaethon," *The Hudson Review* 39, no. 2 (Summer 1986): pp. 234–37.

Works by
Thomas Hardy

The Poor Man and the Lady, (never published) 1868.

Desperate Remedies, (published anonymously) 1871.

Under the Greenwood Tree, 1872.

A Pair of Blue Eyes, 1873.

Far from the Madding Crowd, 1874.

The Hand of Ethelberta, 1876.

The Return of the Native, 1878.

The Trumpet-Major, 1880.

A Laodicean, 1881.

Two on a Tower, 1882.

The Mayor of Casterbridge, 1886.

The Woodlanders, 1887.

Wessex Tales, (short stories) 1888.

Tess of the d'Urbervilles, 1891.

A Group of Noble Dames, (short stories) 1891.

Life's Little Ironies, (short stories) 1894.

Jude the Obscure, 1895.

The Well-Beloved, 1897.

Wessex Poems, 1898.

Poems of the Past and the Present, 1901.

The Dynasts, Part I, (an epic-drama about the Napoleonic Wars) 1903.

The Dynasts, Part II, (an epic-drama) 1906.

The Dynasts, Part III, (an epic-drama) 1908.

Time's Laughingstocks, (poems) 1909.

A Changed Man, (short stories) 1913.

Satires of Circumstance, (poems) 1914.

Selected Poems, 1916.

Moments of Vision, (poems) 1917.

The Famous Tragedy of the Queen of Cornwall, 1923.

Human Shows, (poems) 1925.

Winters Words, (poems) 1928.

The Early Life of Thomas Hardy, (an autobiography) 1928.

The Later Years of Thomas Hardy, 1930.

Works About
Thomas Hardy

Abercrombie, Lascelles. *Thomas Hardy: A Critical Study.* London: M. Secker, 1912.

Berger, Sheila. *Thomas Hardy and Visual Structures: Framing, Disruption, Process.* New York: New York University Press, 1990.

Boumelha, Penny. *Thomas Hardy and Women: Sexual Ideology and Narrative Form.* Sussex; Totowa, New Jersey: Harvester Press; Barnes & Noble, 1982.

Brinkley, Richard. *Thomas Hardy as a Regional Novelist.* St. Peter Port, Guernsey, Channel Islands: Toucan Press, 1968.

Brooke-Rose, Christine. "Ill Wit and Sick Tragedy: *Jude the Obscure.*" *The Alternative Hardy.* Lance St. John Butler, editor. London: Macmillan, 1989: 26–48.

Chew, Samuel C. *Thomas Hardy, Poet and Novelist.* New York: Russell & Russell, 1928.

Clark, Susan L. *Thomas Hardy and the Tristan Legend.* Heidelberg: C. Winter, 1983.

Collins, Deborah L. *Thomas Hardy and His God: A Liturgy of Unbelief.* New York: St. Martin's Press, 1990.

Cox, Reginald Gordon, ed. *Thomas Hardy, The Critical Heritage.* London: Routledge & K. Paul; New York: Barnes & Noble, 1970.

Daleski, Hillel Matthew. *Thomas Hardy and Paradoxes of Love.* Columbia: University of Missouri Press, 1997.

Draper, Jo. *Thomas Hardy's England.* London: J. Cape, 1984.

Elliott, Ralph Warren Victor. *Thomas Hardy's English.* Oxford, England: B. Blackwell in association with Andre Deutsch, 1984

Entice, Andrew. *Thomas Hardy, Landscapes of the Mind.* London: MacMillan Press, 1979.

Gatrell, Simon. *Thomas Hardy and the Proper Study of Mankind.* Charlottesville: University Press of Virginia, 1993.

Gerber, Helmut E., ed. *Thomas Hardy: An Annotated Bibliography of Writings About Him.* De Kalb: Northern Illinois University Press, 1973.

Gibson, James. *Thomas Hardy: A Literary Life*. New York: St. Martin's Press, 1996.

Gittings, Robert. *Thomas Hardy's Later Years*. Boston: Little Brown, 1978.

Goode, John. *Thomas Hardy: The Offensive Truth*. Oxford; New York: B. Blackwell, 1988.

Guerard, Albert J. *Thomas Hardy: The Novels and Stories*. Cambridge, Mass.: Harvard University Press, 1949.

————, ed. *Hardy: A Collection of Critical Essays: Twentieth Century Views*. Englewood Cliffs, N.J., 1963.

Halliday, Frank Ernest. *Thomas Hardy: His Life and Work*. New York: Barnes & Noble, 1972.

Hands, Timothy. *Thomas Hardy: Distracted Preacher?: Hardy's Religious Biography and Its Influence on his Novels*. New York: St. Martin's Press, 1989.

Hardy, Barbara Nathan. *Thomas Hardy: Imagining Imagination: Hardy's Poetry and Fiction*. London; New Brunswick, New Jersey: Athlone Press; Somerset, New Jersey: Distributed in the U.S. by Transaction Publishers, 2000.

Hardy, Evelyn. *Thomas Hardy: A Critical Biography*. New York: St. Martin's Press, 1954.

Hasan, Noorul. *Thomas Hardy: The Sociological Imagination*. London; New York: Macmillan, 1982.

Holland, Clive. *Thomas Hardy, O. M.: The Man, His Works, and the Land of Wessex*. New York: Haskell House, 1966.

Jedrzejewski, Jan. *Thomas Hardy and the Church*. New York: St. Martin's Press, 1996.

Langbaum, Robert Woodrow. *Thomas Hardy in Our Time*. New York: St. Martin's Press, 1995.

Langland, Elizabeth. "Becoming a Man in *Jude the Obscure*." *The Sense of Sex: Feminist Perspectives on Hardy*. Margaret R. Higonnet, editor. Urbana and Chicago: University of Illionis Press, 1993: 32–48.

Lefebure, Molly. *Thomas Hardy's World: The Life, Times and Works of the Great Novelist and Poet*. London: Carlton Books, 1997.

Lerner, Laurence, and John Holmstrom, eds. *Thomas Hardy and His Readers: A Selection of Contemporary Reviews*. New York: Barnes & Noble, 1968.

Lerner, Laurence. *Thomas Hardy's* The Mayor of Casterbridge: *Tragedy or Social History?* London: Published for Sussex University Press by Chatto & Windus, 1975.

Mallett, Phillip. "Sexual Ideology and Narrative Form in *Jude the Obscure.*" *English* 38 (1989): 211–24.

Milberg-Kaye, Ruth. *Thomas Hardy—Myths of Sexuality.* New York: J. Jay Press, 1983.

Miller, J. Hillis. *Thomas Hardy: Distance and Desire.* Cambridge, Massachusetts: Belknap Press of Harvard University Press, 1970.

Millgate, Michael. *Thomas Hardy: A Biography.* New York: Random House, 1982.

———. *Thomas Hardy: His Career as a Novelist.* New York: Random House, 1971.

———, ed. *Letters of Emma and Florence Hardy.* New York: Oxford University Press, 1996.

———, ed. *Thomas Hardy's Public Voice: The Essays, Speeches, and Miscellaneous Prose.* Oxford; New York: Clarendon Press; Oxford University Press, 2001.

Morrell, Roy. *Thomas Hardy: The Will and the Way.* Kuala Lumpur, University of Malaya Press: Sole distributors: Oxford University Press: London and New York, 1968.

O'Sullivan, Timothy. *Thomas Hardy: An Illustrated Biography.* New York: St. Martin's Press, 1976.

Page, Norman, ed. *Thomas Hardy: Family History.* London: Routledge/Thoemmes Press, 1998.

Pinion, F. B., ed. *Thomas Hardy and the Modern World.* Dorchester: Thomas Hardy Society, 1974.

———. *Thomas Hardy: Art and Thought.* Totowa, New Jersey: Rowman and Littlefield, 1977.

———. *A Thomas Hardy Dictionary With Maps and a Chronology.* New York: New York University Press, 1989.

———. *Thomas Hardy: His Life and Friends.* New York: St. Martin's Press, 1992.

Prasad, Suman Prabha. *Thomas Hardy and D. H. Lawrence: A Study of the Tragic Vision in Their Novels.* New Delhi: Arnold-Heinemann Publishers (India), 1976.

Purdy, Richard Little. *Thomas Hardy: A Bibliographical Study.* London and New York: Oxford University Press, 1954.

Robinson, Jeremy. *Thomas Hardy and John Cowper Powys: Wessex Revisited.* Kidderminster, England: Crescent Moon, 2nd ed., 1994.

Rutland, William R. *Thomas Hardy: A Study of His Writings and Their Background.* New York: Russell & Russell, 1962.

Sherrick, Julie. *Thomas Hardy's Major Novels: An Annotated Bibliography.* Lanham, Maryland: Scarecrow Press; Pasadena, California: Salem Press, 1998.

Steward, John Innes Mackintosh. *Thomas Hardy: A Critical Biography.* London: Longman, 1971.

Sumner, Rosemary. *Thomas Hardy, Psychological Novelist.* London: Macmillan, 1981.

Thomas, Jane. *Thomas Hardy, Femininity and Dissent: Reassessing the Minor Novels.* Basingstoke; New York: Macmillan; St. Martin's Press, 1999.

White, Reginald James. *Thomas Hardy and History.* New York: Barnes & Noble, 1974.

Williams, Merryn. *Thomas Hardy and Rural England.* New York: Columbia University Press, 1972.

Wilson, Keith. *Thomas Hardy on Stage.* New York: St. Martin's Press, 1995.

Wotton, George. *Thomas Hardy: A Materialist Criticism.* Totowa, New Jersey: Barnes & Noble, 1985.

Wright, Janet B. "Hardy and His Contemporaries: The Literary Context of *Jude the Obscure*." *Inscape* 14 (1980): 135–50.

Acknowledgments

Babb, Howard. "Setting and Theme in *Far From the Madding Crowd*" *ELH*, Vol. 30, No. 2 (June 1963): pp. 147–49. © 1963 by Johns Hopkins University Press. Reprinted by permission of the Johns Hopkins University Press.

"The Mirror and the Sword: Imagery in *Far From the Madding Crowd*" by Richard C. Carpenter. From *Nineteenth-Century Fiction*, Vol. 18, No. 4 (March 1964): pp. 331–33; 335–36. © 1964 by the Regents of the University of California. Reprinted by permission.

"Androgyny, Survival, and Fulfillment in Thomas Hardy's *Far From the Madding Crowd*" by William Mistichelli. From *Modern Language Studies* Vol. 18, No. 3 (Summer 1988): pp. 53–55. © 1988 by Modern Language Studies. Reprinted by permission.

"*Far From the Madding Crowd* as Modified Pastoral" by Michael Squires. From *Nineteenth-Century Fiction* Vol. 25, No. 3 (December 1970): pp. 299–301; 303. © 1970 by the Regents of the University of California. Reprinted by permission.

"Angles of Vision and Questions of Gender in *Far from the Madding Crowd*" by Judith Bryant Wittenberg. From *The Centennial Review,* Vol. 30, No. 1 (Winter 1986): pp. 25–27. © 1986 by Michigan State University Press. Reprinted by permission.

Darwin's Plots: Evolutionary Narrative in Darwin, George Eliot and Nineteenth-Century Fiction by Gillian Beer (pp. 224–26; 230–33). © 2000 by Cambridge University Press. Reprinted with permission of Cambridge University Press.

"The Quiet Women of Egdon Heath" by Jennifer Gribble. From *Essays in Criticism,* Vol. 46, No. 3 (July 1996): pp. 234–37. © 1996 by Oxford University Press. Reprinted by permission of Oxford University Press.

"Hardy: Versions of Pastoral" by Robert Langbaum. From *Victorian Literature and Culture,* Vol. 20 (1993): pp. 245–47. © 1993 by AMS Press. Reprinted by permission.

"The Magic of Metaphor in *The Return of the Native*" by Charles E. May. From *Colby Library Quarterly,* Vol. 22, No. 2 (June 1986): pp. 111–12; 114–15. © 1986 by Colby Library Quarterly. Reprinted by permission.

Index of
Themes and Ideas

Mrs. d'Urberville in, 97, 105; Eliza Louisa Durbeyfield in, 102, 103, 105; Joan Durbeyfield in, 98, 102, 103, 104, 107; John Durbeyfield in, 97, 102, 104; Tess Durbeyfield in, 12, 97–103, 106–11, 114–20; Tess Durbeyfield's purity in, 108–11, 115; Tess Durbeyfield's recuperation in, 114–17; Tess Durbeyfield's sexuality in, 106–8; Marian, Izz Huett, and Retty Priddle in, 99, 102, 105, 118; maternal imagery in, 108–11; plot summary of, 97–103; psychological reading of recuperative process in, 114–17; Rachel and Leah story in Genesis and Darwin's sexual selection theory in, 117–20; Sorrow in, 99, 105, 111; as tragedy, 12; tragedy of consciousness in, 111–14